Conceived to Lead

DISMANTLING THE GLASS CEILING MINDSET

COMPILED BY

Carla Wynn Hall and CaZ

CZI Publishing
an imprint of
Manifest Publishing

CaZ, Author, Editor, Compiler, Publisher
Carla Wynn Hall, Compiler, Author

Additional Authors:
Jessica Peterson, Foreword   Vicki Ibaugh
Cynthia Beyer   Annette Marie Moore

Additional Authors / Contributors:
Rifat Arif   Coni K. Meyers
Akeh Bernardine   Rachele Millions
Marie Dahl   Rachelle Manieri
Brenda Dempsey   Michelle Molotte
Michelle Den Boer   Dorothy M. Neddermeyer
Lea Durbin   Joy S. Pederson
Annette Fluit   Jacqueline D. Pickering
Elizabeth Hassan   Gloria Grace Rand
Claire Ryan Heatley   Chondra Raye Rankin
Cheryl Jacobs   Susan Robichaud
Stephanie Leivas   Melissa Rodriguez
Roxanne Lynch   Laraine Sacco
Judith Lynne Miller-McKay   Trish Springsteen
Jennifer Elizabeth Masters   Becky Stonebarger
Kavita Melwani

Graphics and Marketing Support from Joshua Mancil,
http://boldimpressionsweb.com/

CZI Publishing - imprint of Manifest Publishing
Conceived to Lead / CaZ —1st ed, CZI Publishing
ISBN-10:1-944913-16-5
ISBN-13:978-1-944913-16-8

Contents

Foreword

JESSICA PETERSON

Achievers say No more than Yes. I do say No a lot. This was not always the case. When I was first asked to write the foreword for the book Conceived to Lead, I had to say Yes!

Why? Because I know this book will shift and change lives.

There are several other reasons I said Yes. First and foremost, the book was being co-authored by one of my favorite students and publisher, CaZ, the Writer Success Coach and owner of Manifest Publishing. She has edited and published several of my books. She is a GEM.

Second, I heard that another one of my students, Cynthia Beyer was to be featured. She absolutely rocks! Cindy is an attorney on mission to empower single moms and give them support.

Carla, who authors the book with CaZ, was recently introduced to me by CaZ. In a short time, I have learned that Carla is a person who really wants to be inspired, desires to make changes in her life, and to make a difference for others. Thank you, Carla for bringing together the outstanding women in this book!

As I read these stories, I could not help but be absolutely inspired! Each woman has a unique story that will shift and change lives. Some have encountered and overcome abuse in school, fibromyalgia, car accidents, cancer, loss of a child, and more. You will relate to at least one of these women leaders. Each has gone through something traumatic that turned their lives to a different path.

I noticed one aspect that remained the same: they find new direction from their challenges and continue on their leadership path. The stories in this book demonstrate how our purpose can start out one way and end up evolving into another path.

I am always listening to messages. Recently I read a story of a man who had chosen a path in his life and then, after listening to what was taking place around him, shifted his path and ended up with a truly blessed life. After five plus years of coaching and consulting individuals and companies about social media, branding, how to network and market, and be productive, I knew it was time to make a bigger difference.

When I experienced a trend of many individuals asking to be instructed and certified by my agency, I listened.

WOW!

Here was the message, loud and clear. This was my way to make a bigger impact in this world. Now I can coach and guide others into leading based on my tools. It is simple; you WOW people, your business grows and you have a prosperous, AKA WOW, life yourself.

After my husband was in ICU, I valued my time even more. When shortly thereafter I experienced Bell's Palsy not once but twice, I was inspired to write a new book, *Create The Perfect Day* and its companion action guide, *Create The Perfect Day Planner*.

These health issues for my family were a message, and I paid attention. Time is our biggest asset and one we can never get back. My purpose is to educate and inspire others to take control of their time because each of us are gifted with only so much of it.

Are you listening to messages and taking action? Are you a leader? Are you scared to step up?

In the book *Purposed Powered People* I spoke about my purpose. I spoke about how it was a sign of what I was called to do when I evaluated what I enjoyed as a kid. I absolutely loved to play Barbies. Each of my dolls had their lives mapped out. They individually had careers, schedules for when they volunteered, what their pay range was, and when they got raises.

I thought this was a normal way to play Barbies until I went to a party and all the girls were playing Barbies differently. Each of their Barbies were married and house wives. This caused me to evaluate my Barbies. None of them were married. They did not strive to be house wives. They had careers. They were fashionistas. (By the way, I won best dressed in high school and I shopped Goodwill.)

Was my view wrong? Were my friends wrong? Not at all. There is nothing wrong with being a house wife or a stay-at-home spouse, let alone being married. Nor is life any less worthy when a career is a part of it.

I was a smart kid, strong on math, and skipped a few grades. It is no surprise I ended up leading in the financial industry. I share this with you because I really want you to reflect on what made you happy as a kid. Those childhood dreams can be a sign of what you are called to do and be; including being a leader.

Sometimes we may not recognize the sign. I recall being asked to speak in front of an audience at school in sixth grade. I turned bright red!!! As the years went on, I kept being asked to speak well into my adult life. I actually went to therapy to learn how to deal with all the speaking requests. Many who know me find this revelation to be shocking since I have spoken to many groups and before hundreds, thousands of people, including TEDx.

You see, I still do not enjoy speaking but now I realize it is part of my calling and purpose. You may be called to lead and it can make you uncomfortable, but listen to the message!

You are not alone. This is one of the reasons I love my mastermind. We all come together to inspire, share our challenges in a safe place, and overcome them. We were created to connect and bond with like-minded people. Relationships are important and I highly suggest you connect with at least one of the women authoring the chapters of *Conceived to Lead*. When we come together to make a difference, big shifts happen.

This book will leave you feeling so inspired that you will evaluate your life. Life is such a beautiful gift. When I work with people and companies on time management, they discover how much can be done when you choose a life with purpose and structure. *Conceived to Lead* will inspire you to take action and quit wasting time. Guaranteed!

After reading this book, may I make a suggestion for you? Please take the time to reflect on your purpose. Evaluate what is next for you. Go out. Find your tribe to take you where you desire and deserve to be.

Yes, that is right. I said *desire and deserve*. Often in my conversations with amazing women I discover they have confidence issues or feel uncertain that they deserve the best. In my book, *Create The Perfect Day*, I talk about how every day is perfect because you are alive.

Create a life you desire and deserve, live it and love it! Go find your tribe and lead.

ABOUT JESSICA PETERSON

As the Founder of the Simply WOW Agency and Customer WOW Project. Jessica has a highly successful background in banking, mortgage, finance and insurance that prepared her well to lead an equally successful agency. She has a passion for numbers and simplifying processes and brings her unique skills to bear for clients, often propelling them to achieve heights in their business that they had not previously envisioned.

As an author, Jessica has five books currently available. *Purpose Powered People, Forty and Wiser: Remarkable Insider Secrets from Women 40 and Wiser,* and *Entrepreneurs: Instantly Create 9 Weeks of Time Off!* are the three most recent.

She is one of the Founders of *Contractor Success Training* and *Mortgage Prosperity Academy*.

Jessica guides Simply WOW Agency to serve these industries:

- Coaches
- Mortgage Professionals
- Real Estate Agents and Agencies
- Insurance Professionals
- Financial Advisors
- Contractors
- Companies who have innovative solutions to serve and positively impact lives

---

Connect with Jessica

Website: http://www.simplywowagency.com
Facebook: https://www.facebook.com/simplywowagency

Preface

LEAD HER SHIP

CARLA WYNN HALL, COMPILER

When pondering on what I would write about for this book, the word leadership had a sting to it. Not a hard sting, but one that I could not put my finger on or wrap my head around.

I thought, "I have never been on a stage. I have never led a massive movement. How can I be a leader?".

Then I started to think back through times when I led my family, I led other women, I led through hardships, and most importantly, I led myself out of rock bottom.

It hit me then that I am a *Leader of my Ship* and the theme Lead Her Ship percolated in my mind.

Leadership is a rather dominate word and one that conjures up thoughts of rulers, government officials, and dictators. Even though Leadership is a trait which is present among us all, in all walks of life women in particular are taught that it's unladylike to take on too much leadership.

I have lead more than one thousand women through books just like this. I have typed out chapters for women who were dyslexic so they could become published. I work with 2 women who have cerebral palsy to help them stay busy writing. I have endured criticism and haters like you would never imagine. I have published a 16-year boy and his mom in an anthology where he discussed, for the first time, thoughts of suicide he had when his mom married an abusive man. I have helped women who could not speak about being raped in the military to write out their story; to strip down the memory and thrive.

I am a leader. I am a born leader. I want to lead. I desire to lead. I will not ever stop leading women and girls and helping them to get beyond any feeling of being limited.

I am a leader.

You are a leader.

The theme of this book is Leadership. *Conceived to Lead* means *Born to Lead*. Women are a driving force in this world. Our goal is to deny the myth. Our need is to change the mindset. Our message is to expose the truth. There is no ceiling, of any sort, that stops our ability to lead.

Introduction

CAZ, EDITOR AND PUBLISHER

Why have you chosen to read this book? What about the title, Conceived to Lead, appeals to you? Are you a friend or relative of one of the chapter authors? Are you amid your own journey to fill your leadership shoes?

I do not know your answers to these questions. Whatever your answer, what I do know is that you are a seeker of knowledge and a person who wants to understand more about the roles we choose to play during the short time we're on this Earth.

When Carla Wynn Hall came to me with the concept of this book, I felt an immediate attraction to the subject. I do believe we are all born with leadership ability. It is through the choices we make and the choices imposed upon us by our life situation that our leadership ability is either nurtured or drops into disuse.

This book is a collection of stories, essays, and lessons from women who have chosen to wield and hone their leadership abilities;

amazing women who have learned (or intuitively known) how to turn adversity into achievement.

Rifat Arif (Sister Zeph) leads an organization for girls in a very rough country. Her leadership is massive and to be saluted.

Vicki Ibaugh shows busy entrepreneurs how to experience true freedom by creating courses and programs that allow them to have more time, money and impact.

Michelle Molotte leads women into their individual power, to live life according to their desire.

Akeh Bernardine is a leader among women who have had tragic relationships, been harmed, hurt and abused, by showing them their beauty and power.

Annette Marie Moore believes your health is your most important asset and helps women kick the diet mentality to adopt a wholehearted, healthy lifestyle.

Cynthia Beyer is an attorney who coaches single parents to raise children as leaders who will impact the world in a positive way.

Liz Hassan is Mum to the whole world and gives new meaning to leadership through caregiving on both a professional and personal level.

These are but a few of the women leaders who authored chapters in this book. We hope you enjoy reading Conceived to Lead and learning more about these amazing women. Their stories are poignant. Their lessons are real. Their words are true.

"...if I have a daughter I will tell her she can do anything, and I will mean it, because I have no other intention of informing her otherwise. As my mother did with me, and my mother's mother before her, I shall simply hide the truth from her. I will tell her that despite what others may whisper, there is no difference between her and any boy. I will tell her to work her hardest and try her best. And that if one day she looks around and finds that, despite her very best efforts, lesser men have superseded her, then she probably could have done better.

These words may not be true, nor will they be fair, but I would hope that they ensure she never becomes a victim of her own femininity. I hope she will be empowered to pick herself up, study harder, work longer, and exceed her own expectations.

I don't want my daughter to break any glass ceilings. I'd rather she never even contemplated their existence. Because glass ceilings, closed doors, and boys clubs are notions, they're ideas, and they're not tangible. You can't see, touch, or feel them. They can only exercise power over us if we choose to believe in them. So why lay down your own gauntlet?

The cliché rings true, if you reach for the moon, you might just land on the stars. Throw a glass ceiling into the works, and it can only get in the way.

And I suspect that deep down, every woman who ever truly excelled thought exactly this way. I doubt they ever gave much thought to the fact that they are women. I think they just really wanted to rock out. And they did; louder, harder, and better than anyone else around them. And at some point down the line, enough people took note."

~ Amy Mowafi, Fe-mail 2

"The Gift of Inspiring Others to Fully Step into their Best Self through Daily Rebirth of Body, Mind, and Soul." ~ Michelle Den Boer

Bossy Little Girl Becomes a Leader

MICHELLE DEN BOER

*E*ver since I was a little girl, I have always been a leader. Have you ever seen the Facebook meme that says something along the lines of a bossy little girl becomes a leader? Well, I am pretty sure that meme was created for me. Not only do I have a calling to be a leader, I have a desire to motivate and help others become their best version of themselves.

For as long as I can remember, I wanted to make the best of myself. I was one of those women who was determined to do it all!

My picture of a successful woman is a great mother who has a great career. She is proactive with her children, does it all, and does it well! When my son was seven years old, I was working in a law firm as a paralegal. I also helped in my son's classroom once a week, was an assistant coach for my son's soccer team, and still managed to be a wife, a friend, and a sister. I loved to plan get-togethers with friends, to go have my nails and hair done, and go to coffee with co-workers. You know, the fun things that us women do.

In just minutes it all changed and life as I and my family knew changed. I was in a horrible car accident. My brakes went out. I rear-ended a stopped bus with my car going 35 miles per hour.

When I regained consciousness, I heard my son crying, "Are you ok, mommy?" His voice was scared and terrified as he cried. I had hit my head on the steering wheel and he didn't know if I was ok. I pushed to open my door, and it was stuck. I couldn't get it to open.

My son was quietly crying, but it was a cry I had never heard come from him before. I felt a panic as I continued to struggle to get us out of my car. I could not reach him in in the back without getting out of the car. To this day, I don't know where the strength came from, but without thinking I kicked and pushed and the door opened.

As I moved to get out, the emergency team suddenly appeared in front of me. I heard them say, as if from a distance, to stay still and that they will help me get my son. I didn't even listen. My focus was on my son. I asked him if he was ok. He said yeah, but he was scared and I held his hand until the team got to us. Finally, I was able to un-buckle him and grab him in my arms. I have never been so relieved to hold him and know he was ok.

It wasn't until that point that I realized the damage that had been done to my car. I started to feel sore muscles and my head hurt. I fig-ured we both should be examined by a doctor. The doctor did a full examination of both of us. Thank goodness, my son was totally fine.

I had no idea the damage I had done to my body. I began feeling more and more pain. It was an odd feeling I had never felt before. I was just all around exhausted. The doctor prescribed painkillers and muscle relaxers. Once we were home and my son was sleeping, I took the medicine and I was able to sleep. I slept hard through the night. About 4 am I woke up with pain that was unbelievably excruciating.

This was only the beginning. The pain did not go away. I went to chiropractic care, massage therapy, and stayed on pain medications. All I did was sleep. Between the pain meds making me tired, the pain in itself, and my body trying to heal itself—sleep was all I could man-age. I couldn't get enough sleep.

Those of you who have kiddos know how hard it is to entertain a 7-year-old while you sleep. I was no longer able to help in my son's classroom and thank goodness, we were on a break from soccer. And then there were all the medical appointments I was attending. Between the exhaustion and pain, I felt like my life was over.

After going through this for a few months with no change, one day the doctor said we needed to discuss a diagnosis. She diagnosed me with fibromyalgia. Now, at this time I knew only one person with fibromyalgia. And I flashed right away on how sick she would get. I remembered all the times she wasn't able to get out of bed and when I helped take care of her children. So, to me this was a horrible, life altering diagnosis.

I know it could've been way worse but I'm an active person and I knew my life would not work well with the pain, exhaustion, and anxiety as well as all the other things that come along with fibromyalgia. I asked her what we could do to handle this as natural a way as possible and still get back my quality-of- life. She connected me with a therapist who actually help me discuss all kinds of different pain management options as well as taught me important skills for self-care.

Turns out, I have a low tolerance to medications. The pain meds just knocked me out. I knew that medication wasn't going to be a permanent solution, especially since I am determined to be active and enjoy doing things with my child. However, the pain, and exhaustion was so bad. I had to find a way to manage it and still function.

I began slowly with yoga and a healthy diet. At first, I was totally wiped out after taking only part of a yoga class. I was so determined that this had to work that I made myself last longer each time I went to class. After class, I would soak my muscles in a hot bath to keep from being too sore. There were days I took three hot baths to manage the pain from the workout or fibro. Can you imagine what you feel like after a very tough intense workout for the very first time? It was like that but, worse.

As I continued to push through the pain, overtime I could tell that yoga was working. I felt a bit better and not quite as sore. I decided to step up my activity and begin full body training with weights. It was amazing. I continued and work slowly and eventually my body didn't hurt as much and I wasn't as tired. I still needed to nap during the day but it was only a short one. I was getting some of my energy back.

The more I worked out, ate healthy, and really took care of myself, the better I felt. This felt amazing, I was beginning to be myself again. I was so excited that I decided to study to get my personal training certification to understand to how and why this was working. The other major key was learning accountability as well remaining a balanced life. Even people at the gym saw the differences in me and asked me questions. They wanted to know what I did differently. The changes were unbelievable to them and soon I was training people.

Now I realize that helping my clients experience amazing life changing health journeys is more than a physical workout. I realized I actually do more than train bodies, I mentor them to live a healthier, more balanced life.

The worst day of my life has come full circle. I will never be the person I was before the car accident. And that is good because my journey to health has allowed me to reaffirm my own leadership abilities and even more, help others find their own way.

One of the worst days of my life was a blessing in many ways. I am firm believer that everything happens for a reason and the experiences we have are what make us who we are today. I personally look at my diagnosis of fibro as having my own built in accountability.

The car accident has changed my life and lead me full circle to my passion of being a leader to help others live a healthier, happier, more balanced life.

AUTHOR MICHELLE DEN BOER

A Fitness/Wellness Mentor, Inspirational Speaker, and Author, Michelle's background is as a Personal Trainer who motivates and helps others become healthy. Recently, she led her local community in a yearlong challenge to become healthier. Being healthy is more than a workout and a diet to Michelle, it is a way of life.

Within the process of her own personal growth, she has developed the Den Stability Ball, the most effective tool available to help individuals live a well-balanced life. This awe-inspiring mentorship program, offers the nine facets of life and includes a powerful process and the motivation to move individuals to action while they gain the ability to strategize, set goals, and be held accountable. Den Stability Ball has the potential to breakthrough any obstacles that may be standing in the way of living an inspiring journey of growth, happiness and health!

Connect with the Author . . .

Website: http://www.denstrong.com
Social Media
  Facebook: https://www.facebook.com/MichelleLDenBoer
  Instagram: https://www.instagram.com/michelle_denstrong/
  Twitter: https://twitter.com/DenStrongMentor

"Illiteracy is darkness and education is light and I was born to transform darkness into light." ~ Sister Zeph

Teach Our Girls Being a Leader is Not Being Naughty

RIFAT ARIF (SISTER ZEPH)

I was a naughty girl—at least by the society standard used to judge appropriate behavior for women. I was a leader in my school. I wanted to be a lawyer; I wrote my first article on women's rights at age 13 in a famous newspaper called *Daily Jung of Pakistan*.

My mother, like every mother in my country, used to tell me that one day I would get married. I always kept thinking no—God has not sent me into this world only to get married. My heart always told me that it wasn't so. I was a dreamer and wanted to fly high. My lifestyle was different; I always wanted to explore what was different.

And yet, I was also sensitive. I left my school in seventh grade and decided to never go back to school again because of one incident that changed my life forever. My heart felt humiliated, I cried for many days. I wanted to die, and I did not see anyone for days. I felt like my heart was dying inside me.

The incident began innocently. The teacher was out of the room and I decided to deliver a speech to my class, acting like a teacher. I was standing on the teacher's chair. When she came into the room, she beat me for this in front of my classmates. She abused me and the girls made fun of me. I cried and cried. I was hurt mentally.

Then I stopped crying and decided to surprise them all. I did something that nobody expected; I chose to leave school. All at once life changed. It seemed, at least to my parents, that all dreams were over. My parents tried to force me to join another school, but I did not.

As young as I was, I understood that leaving school did not mean that I stopped studying. I read in my home privately, and began to teach other girls, although I never took any tuition. It was during this time that I decided to teach and to treat girls with the respect, love, and care that I was not given in my school. I decided to start a school.

I made home visits in my village. I made pamphlets to distribute among people. I promised free education. I walked even further to tell about my school in the nearby villages. I did everything I could think of to convince the people to send their girls to my school. I told them that I would teach them English for free. I visited people with my mother on every Sunday, but no one was ready.

I was not taken seriously. It was funny, a joke for some of the people around me. No one trusted me and no one was ready to join my school because I was just 13 years old. But I kept going, I wanted no child to experience what had happened to me.

I did not give up. I was determined to create a school where a stick would never be used and where education would be interesting for the children. In beginning, there was only one student. We started, and for many years remained, in open air. It was not until 2014 that we had a building. We began with no rooms, no pen, no copy machine, and only a few books. In summer, we sat under the sun. In winter, we sat under blankets. And when it rained, we had to leave our studies. Our roof was the sky. We rejoiced when we had normal weather so we could study in open air and accepted that sometimes we could not.

At age sixteen I did my matriculation and started a job as a receptionist in a telecom franchise where I was being paid 15$ a month. I used my salary to buy stationary and other important things for my school. Since then I have continued to work, continued with my own education, and to run my school. I did a Masters in Political science in 2010, and Masters in History in 2013. All of my education was achieved with no institution or teacher's help, only with self-studies.

And then my world changed: I joined social media in 2011. I saw the potential and posted about our work daily. Soon, people from around the world followed, and gave me support, both moral and financial.

In 2014, I won Lynn Syms Global prize from World Pulse USA, in 2015 Channel News Asia Singapore made a documentary on my life (Flight of the Falcons), in 2016 this film won a Gold Medal from New York film festival, in 2016 I became Swedish Institute alumna after joining Young Connectors of Future program in Sweden, in 2017 I became Aluma of EWHA Women University after joining 12th EGEP.

Through social media and these global social programs, we gathered enough funds to build a small school building. In two rooms, we teach 106 girls and give them 12 years of free education. At our stitching center, 80 women a year are learning to sew and the craft of stitching. At our beauty salon training center, 60 women are becoming professional beauticians. Our computer center teaches technology skills to 60 girls. Each year, our English Language Center 60 girls are immersed in listening to English and learn to speak, write, and read English. We also teach self-defense techniques, basketball, and boxing. We are truly global as teachers from USA, Europe, and India give lessons through Skype.

We have taught and empowered thousands of girls and women during two decades. Our students have gone on to be teachers, nurses, administrators, business ladies, and university and college students. They learn to drive cars. They work among men with no fear. They support their families and feed their children. Our students have been shown a different world. They are changing the concept (still present in our society) that women depend on men for their needs.

I am immensely proud of the women who have attended our school and who understand what it means to be empowered and treated with respect. And who know what it means to treat our sisters with equal respect. For myself, I have been working in a large organization for 18 years even as I ran the school. I am the administrator of a world-wide women's community page on Facebook and I administer my own page, Zephaniah Free Education. I also write articles to post on websites about the issues women face in my part of the world.

I continue to study and am learning journalism. And I produce theatrical info-dramas in my community to provide messages of peace and respect for women and the importance of education for all.

My focus remains on my part of the world where we need to continue to improve education. It is only the beginning of my work.

Every day, I see women who suffer all their life, who are being tortured mentally and physically, who are not being given an education, who are not empowered, who are locked into child marriage, and who are the victims of honor killings. These are the challenges we face and the injustices we must end.

When I look at the condition and helplessness of these women, it gives me the spirit to go ahead, to never stop, simply to keep going.

I know there is only one solution to all our problems, and that is education and awareness of our rights. I want every girl to be educated, empowered, and protected. For this I will keep fighting throughout my life.

AUTHOR RIFAT ARIF

The following was written by Malee Kenworthy who is a US liaison for Sister Zeph's humanitarian movement.

Leadership to me means that you have someone's back no matter what. Leadership is not just about leading people and having them follow you. I used to have so many misconceptions about leadership before I met Sister Zeph.

March 2015

I met Sister Zeph, a human rights activist, teacher, and school owner in rural Pakistan on the border of India. I met her through Facebook when I was at work one evening. I found her because I was following Malala Yousafzai's page and Malala posted Sister Zeph's documentary. I saw that Sister Zeph was online, and I reached out to her immediately.

What followed was a true and beautiful blossoming of friendship across continents and oceans! Not only did I get close to her but I also go close to the girls at her school because I was teaching them via Skype every weekend. At first, I taught art and then moved to other subjects. Soon, I started helping her fundraise and do marketing.

One year later I went to Pakistan for one month. I had an amazing time. I got to meet the girls, see beautiful sites, meet amazing people, eat yummy food, and do lots of shopping at the bazars.

Looking back over the past two and one-half years of helping this woman and her school, I can see more clearly what leadership is. Through Sister Zeph I see clearly what a true leader is. She is selfless and doesn't let any obstacle stop her. No matter what happens, even if the obstacle and challenges seem like too much to bear, she keeps pressing forward. I have learned much through my humanitarian work. Leadership is all about team work.

Connect with the Author . . .

Foundation: https://zepheducation.org/

"Leadership is the ability to take responsibility for your life by striving to live an authentic life, excelling in every area of your life to the best of your ability, as well as supporting others in finding their path and being the front runners of their lives." ~ Akeh Bernardine

The Power of Self Leadership

PAIN TO RICHES THROUGH SELF-LEADERSHIP:
DIVINE TRANSFORMATION OF YOUR MONEY AND
RELATIONSHIP STORIES VIA SELF-LEADERSHIP.

AKEH BERNARDINE

*D*o you have money and love issues? Have these issues held you down for a long time? I have found this to be true for many women and especially true for those I help. In my profession, I help women to get out of difficult situations, but that is only the first step.

Some women have issues around difficult relationships with men. Their relationship is often so complicated that they've given up and just live their lives with no satisfaction or joy. These women also express that no one day passes without them looking at themselves to cast blame; they believe the problem is with them.

I am originally from Africa, a country called Cameroon. I am currently living in the UK. Can you imagine the challenges I have had in life? I grew up in poverty, with poor health facilities, barely meeting my educational needs, and living in an environment where the girl child or woman is looked upon as a second-class citizen.

My lines and boundaries were blurred. And yet, I am today writing this work—a task beyond the ability of thousands, perhaps millions, of women around the world.

So how do we use self-leadership to help women to dream and achieve their dreams? How do we use self-leadership to transform relationships? You may start by asking, "What is my Divine purpose?"

For me, my Divine purpose is to support women to stop hiding behind the mask of strength and power to start living authentic lives.

For many of us women, we show up in the world pretending that everything is going well, especially regarding money and relationship issues. Many women find it difficult to blow the trumpet to say they've had enough. Is this you, or are you ready to transform? Will you take the blinders from your eyes and live an authentic life?

Many women admire role models such as millionaire entrepreneurs and celebrities. A role model is good. However, you may be surprised to learn that having money and status does not mean you are living your true life. A lot of these women are living fake lives and keep chasing things that they were never called to do, or at the very least they do not incorporate their life purpose into their business or career.

These women achieve almost everything in a material way, but still are empty and don't understand the reason for their creation. These women (men fall prey to this as well) are not living their Divine purpose. They have a blind ambition to make lots of money and have fame. They are hollow, like empty vessels. The noise they make is not real. They hurt inside.

Is there hope for them? And for you? Yes. It is found in Divine transformation, where your relationship stories and money stories are transformed, giving each person the ability to live a fulfilled life.

I am very much touched by women who have had relationship issues where they've been abused emotionally, physically, and sexually and have been left with terrible bruises that continue to have a significant impact on their functioning.

You may ask what does self-leadership have to do with this? I am a case scenario. In my past, I looked up to outstanding women. When I faced hurdles in my life, or when I was in a dark place, these women did not help me.

I believe my place in the world is not to be a woman who sits at home dependent on the man. Whilst growing up, my environment was poverty. Money was an issue, food was a problem. I had no pocket allowance and have always worked to earn my own money to escape poverty. In Africa where I came from children grow into adulthood continuing to depend on their parents. They may blame this on the economy, but I was never like that. I work and make my own money. I do what I have to do. When I was younger, that meant selling old clothes, selling traditional farm produce, selling cooked groundnuts, and carrying goods for sale on my hair. I was not child sitting at home waiting for others to make things happen for me.

But one thing that was an issue was my belief that my parents or my siblings owed me something and that they needed to help me. Although I was achieving, it was not enough. I wanted more. I continued to be miserable—because I believed that someone needed to help me.

I fought for myself, I did what I had to do. But I was not appreciating my achievements. I had the mindset to work hard to achieve, which is a good mindset, but it was not enough. One day, I realized that it must change my mindset or I would never achieve all that I could or all that I was meant to achieve.

I remember the times I was at secondary school from the age of 11 when I started living by myself and had to fend for myself. I learned then how to be accountable for myself. I could look after myself—shopping and cooking my own food and making sure that I attended school—without any adult supervision.

At this young age, I witnessed horrible things happening to my mates. Some were having unprotected sex and ending up with unwanted pregnancies. These were intelligent girls whose choice was children they could not raise or crude abortions and the risk of death due to no medical facilities or not being able to have the money to go to the hospital. The choice was complicated by the fact that abortion was not legalized in my country of origin, Cameroon.

I could start seeing the concepts of self-leadership in play. Because I was, at a very young age, taking responsibility for myself. No one was supporting me, and as I was highly favored by the Divine, I sailed through this period without any mishap. I observed other young people getting drunk, but I did not go down that road.

Thirty Days to a Harmonious Partner Relationship

The only thing stepping between you and your greatness is you. Do you believe this?

Whilst being an adult I made silly decisions around relationships because I wasn't aware of the excruciating consequences on my life at that period. I was more of a follower, being drawn into relationships because I saw everyone else around me in one and I thought I needed a relationship. Well, you know what happened, next, I became a single mother for my 2 children. Not only did I have relationship issues to deal with, at one point I was homeless, jobless and with no support.

Now tell me, who amongst those women top leaders I was looking up to saved me or supported me? None. I therefore do not look up to mystery women who are all making it. I do not believe the talk they are trying to flush down my throat. I do not believe their talk about changing lives of women with the view of replicating their success.

Have you have dwelled on the problems in your marriage for too long and done nothing about it to change your situation? Do you blame your partner and think that constantly reminding him and shouting about the things you go through will change him?

How does that work out for you both? He does not change. You do not change. You are stuck in a circle and holding yourself back. Stop procrastinating. Put the beautiful life you were created to live first.

Everyone has unique gifts, talents, and a purpose that they've been called to. The women whose stories appeal to me are the everyday women on the streets, the ordinary women. These are the women who have consistently supported me. I have received support from family, friends, and neighbors, but most importantly, my success in life has been due to my ability to hold onto hope and consistently be aware that there must be a better way out. It was when I adopted this attitude that I started really living the concepts of self-leadership, throwing away all the mask of pretending all is going well, and striving to live a truthful and authentic life.

I came to know that I am the only one capable of changing my situation. I knew that I must dedicate time and effort to change my circumstances because no one would do it for me. One of the things that helped me were affirmations from the biblical point of view. I strongly believe that as a human being I do not have power to change my situation because when I try that I always fail. I therefore use principles from the Holy Bible and they work magic for me. I meditate on them day and night. The concepts of affirmation became real to me and are very powerful as I am divinely led.

My concepts of self-leadership are built around Divine guidance because of the results that it has produced in my life. These same principles I have used to support women to take control of their lives. I have witnessed the great changes in their lives through our efforts.

Self-leadership is how you can influence your own motivation, cognition, and behavior. It is with this that I will like to share a few of the concepts that have been producing results not only to me but to many other women I have been working with.

You may have children and are the main earner for your family.

You may have had relationship failures and experienced hardship.

You may struggle to care for yourself or for your children.

None of that matters.

I am here to tell you, to show you the way. If a girl from Africa can break the poverty mindset and now live the life that she has dreamed of for years, you too can. I want to let you know that healing and recovering everything you lost is possible.

I teach a 6-week course for women to show you how to transform your life via self-leadership. In this chapter, I will share a part of this course. I teach women to transform their lives using a journal, doing the work, and watching their transformation.

Week 1: *Position yourself as the best version of you.*

- Identify fears, worries, and pain points.
- Let go of the past and break through what's holding you back.
- Understand the difference between the feminine inner-self and feminine outer-self function and the importance of making decisions from your feminine inner self.

Week 2: *Highlight immediate and future dangers.*

- Articulate the immediate and future dangers are for your life if you remain in the same situation.
- Identify the complicating factors that inhibit your progress.

Week 3: *Total cleansing process.*

- Using various methods, delete the old files and hurt in your feminine inner-self.
- Living your life from a conscious perspective and understanding the 3 types of consciousness.

Week 4: *Transformation.*

- Be crystal clear about your strengths and weaknesses.
- Replace your feminine inner-self with qualities and values that will take you to the next level of fulfilment.
- Restore dignity and feminine power.

Week 5: Be clear about your boundaries.

- Understand your needs, wants, values, and requirements.
- Know your negotiable and nonnegotiable requirements.
- Be clear about your needs.
- Say yes to your needs and desires without guilt.

Week 6: Goal setting and accountability.

- Design an action plan and implement strategies learned.
- Set your top five goals and meet your targets.

Experience profound pleasure and joy in every aspect of your life

You are responsible for making the difference for your life, I cannot do it for you, only you can. I can only give you directives and guidance. Change is in your hands. It is not with the role models you are looking up to, not from your parents, not from your husband, family or friends. Only you can change your situation. Stop behaving inappropriately and blaming others for your circumstances.

You need to invest 100 percent in leading your life and being at peace with every area of your life. Accept what you cannot control and learn not to worry. You should be self-aware and be clear about what your values, gifts, and strengths are. You should manage your emotions and weaknesses.

Many women struggle and are confused because they lack the understanding that self-leadership means not really looking up to anyone, but that you excel to the best of your ability and potential. You can do whatever you were put on this earth to do. It is up to you to make sure that you achieve that purpose and your mission.

Speak Truth and be Mindful of the Consequences.

I really like talking to women about discovering their purpose and living a fulfilled life. It is terrible to live unfilled, just dancing on the time of others and not doing that for which you were created. Bring yourself into it.

My vision is a world where every woman is a leader who speak truths and is mindful of the consequences. Every woman deserves to live an authentic life. Every woman deserves to understand, experience, and choose self-leadership.

A leader is comfortable in her own skin. She can live an authentic life of knowing who she is and speaking out from a place of inner strength. A leader takes responsibility for her own life, even if much of the external control is not in her hands. She avoids blame, both self-blame and projecting blame, for her circumstances onto others. She is assertive, lives an authentic life, and believes all things are possible.

How do you become this kind of leader?

I did it. So can you.

Be active. Get things done and don't wait for others to do for you. Achieve what you set out to do.

Do not compare yourself to anyone else because you are unique. Be fair and strong and humble.

Remember that being a self-leader, you look up to yourself. Role models are a tool, not an aspiration. Excel to the best of your ability and know you are enough. Be a woman who listens to your inner soul instead of allowing others to make decisions for you.

When looking back on my life, what advice will I give myself? Nobody owes me anything. My parents, my friends, they owe me nothing. A leader is mindful of the effect her actions have on other people. I did not get to where I am today by myself. I thank God Almighty for giving me the strength and direction for my life, for this piece of work. I thank my husband, children, parents, and siblings who have been supportive.

I took my life into my hands and I am making the best of the it. Take your life into your hands. And remember that wealth alone is not success. Achieve all that you can in life and be sure to fill your soul with purpose and love.

How? Start by healing your wounds and your relationships to discover your purpose. You may have had some hardships in life coupled
with relationship problems. The truth is that money and time and relationships are not your problem. The truth is that money and time
and relationships are not your problem. You may have made many excuses about why you have given up in healing yourself and knowing
your purpose. If to, then you are your worst enemy.

Stop listening to the little voice in you that says you are not good
enough. Do not believe negative self-talk or what other people say
about you. Their main job may be to destroy you. Your main job is to
build yourself up and live your life with purpose.

Understand your purpose, achieve your goals, and live the life you
deserve. Only you can lead yourself to make these changes. No one
can do it for you. You just need little guidance. I am here. Reach out
and I will help you discover the power of self-leadership

AUTHOR AKEH BERNARDINE

I am a wife, and a mother to two lovely boys. I am a qualified social worker in the UK, with a BSc in Social Sciences and a Certificate in Family focused practice. I am a Life & Relationship Coach and Women's Leader who focuses on teaching women how to dream and achieve their goals by using the concepts of self-leadership and accountability from other women.

I have written this chapter for women who are aware that they have goals to achieve regarding their lives, relationships and business and are stock. It is to demonstrate that you can be nothing and by understanding and using the power of self-leadership, your life could quickly turn around in the shortest possible time.

Connect with the Author. . .

Course: https://www.akehb.com/healingrelationshipwounds/
Social Media
  Facebook: https://www.facebook.com/AkehB/
  Facebook: https://www.facebook.com/AkehBernardine/
  YouTube: https://www.youtube.com/chan-nel/UCWdNHL2TvPLpRqii7rRURFA?view_as=subscriberfacebook.com/

"Leadership is having the courage and confidence to evolve, transform, and expand beyond the limiting beliefs of themselves and others, so that we may have a profound and inspiring impact." ~ Melissa Rodriguez

Leadershift:
The Evolution of a Natural Born Leader

MELISSA RODRIGUEZ

*T*his story is for the women of the world who are confined and held to the standards of a small-minded society of limiting beliefs and old school traditions. For the women who want more and are told that they were too much, or to do less. For the women who are suppressed, put down, degraded, belittled, and made to feel like they were at the bottom, and climbed all the way to the top, against the storm of people who wanted nothing more than to watch you fall.

Take a deep breath. Embrace your surroundings. Look into the Universe beyond—it is finally in sight.

You are the leader of *your* life, and you walked, strutted, and stomped your way to this moment. I salute you; I congratulate you, and I welcome you with loving and open arms.

I Was Always a Leader

I was born into a traditional Hispanic family as the eldest of three, with my two younger siblings being brothers. From the moment I came into this world, I was active, smart, hyper, and vocal. Speaking came early for me as did an incredible eagerness and curiosity. My family has pictures of me using my first V-tech (a cute little laptop from the 80s and early 90s) when I was too young to read the keyboard. I was bold and opinionated and nothing or nobody could stop me from vocalizing my thoughts or defending them! Or so I thought.

Society doesn't exactly welcome intelligent women with open arms. When you're smarter than some of your teachers, or at least more open to outside the box ideas, you are told you're wrong even if you're right. What teacher wants to admit that their happy, curious student proved them wrong?

That experience first came about for me in fourth grade when I corrected my teacher. She projected her feelings of embarrassment and shame onto me and bullied me the entire school year. I spent that year in fear, my eagerness to learn deadened, and aware that my knowledge, that even being vocal, would get me into trouble. That was when I decided to normalize myself to fit into what was socially acceptable for a young lady.

Halfway through the fifth-grade school year, my family moved to a new town in the same state. When I enrolled in school, they had me take a test to evaluate where I was academically. The test revealed that I should be placed in their advanced program but it was too late in the year, and I went into the standard academic curriculum. I felt isolated and rejected. I was the new kid, and I feared showing my intelligence in a room full of people I just met.

My fears were validated. It was not long before I was bullied for being the smart girl in a normal classroom. I received high grades on every test and earned the nicknames of *Walking Dictionary* and *Talking Computer*. I was degraded for my intelligence and made to believe that smart is unattractive and that nobody wants to be with or around a nerd. No matter how hard I tried to keep it to myself, there was no way to hide it, my intelligence and a need to share my knowledge naturally flowed out of me.

In middle school, I first experienced a weird, repeating dream about this woman fighting demons on a playground. The dream starts with her watching over the children laughing and playing. Then suddenly she hurries the children away from monsters and evil creatures that are running after them.

I witness her fight with the monsters, on her own. Her power, agility, and speed is intense and makes me feel strong, too. The dream ends with her standing in triumph over the evil creatures, and yet I awake fearful and exhausted.

At first, I didn't know what to think. I shrugged it off as a bad dream, and didn't tell anyone about it, because they would say, "It was a nightmare, nothing to worry about. It's not real."

Something inside me said different because it *felt* real. It felt like I was there, witnessing this woman, witnessing these evils. I was scared of how real it felt.

The dream continued for years, and each time I had this dream, I woke up in that intense fear, in that intense state of exhaustion, as if the battle I was watching her fight was my own.

As I got older, I looked into the meaning of dreams and came to believe this was my subconscious way of dealing with my own demons. Maybe this was my mind telling me to stand up for myself and fight; to defend myself against the evils of the world and society. I did just that. Only it made things worse. Rather than being intelligent, I became a smart, feisty, and aggressive bitch that nobody liked.

It wasn't until I began my spiritual journey that the pieces of my past led to an amazing realization: the woman was not a symbol, she was a past life. She was me, in another time and place. She was a warrior, a fighter, a protector of the innocent. The more I learned about her, the more I realized she was a leader in her own time.

I was *always* a leader.

Pandora's Box—Releasing My Gifts

I've held a semi-successful career for twelve years. When I was 17-years-old, I started to work in a grocery store where I received compliments and positive feedback that I was quick, friendly, and approachable. I listened to my customer's concerns and acted to give them a solution. As I quickly moved up from cashier to customer service desk to front end supervisor, I was asked to take part in the manager's training program. I was a full-time college student, only 19-years-old, and I had a big decision to make: it was either do the program and take time off from school, or finish school and miss out on an opportunity to further my career.

I went to my parents for guidance. Traditional Hispanic family *rules* dictate that your goal is to become better than your parents. Expectations are high, you must finish school and get a degree, so that you can get a better paying job. The oldest takes care of the family, and I was the oldest, so it would be my responsibility to take my parent's place, or to take care of them when they can no longer take care of themselves. And you will not do that as a manager in a grocery store. So, I put my leadership skills in a box, and continued with school.

There's a huge gap between a front-end manager and a salaried manager at the store where I worked. I was maxed out at $8.25 an hour and knew independence would only come by finding a different job. My search brought me to Staples where I interviewed for their Customer Service position. During my interview process, the hiring manager said he wanted to try something different and offered me a place in their Copy and Print Center. I was up for the challenge and took the job.

CPC at Staples is my favorite out of all the jobs I've held. It was here where I put my best gifts forward and learned truly useful skills. I learned how to create brochures, booklets, pamphlets and marketing materials. I learned how to upsell and cross sell. I learned about business and about branding. I learned how to connect with people on a deeper level, asking them more intimate questions about what they do and what they're looking for. I was fast, efficient, and provided my customers with quick and easy business solutions. When I transferred to the store closest to me, the store manager there said that I was a powerhouse associate, and that I was a natural, versatile, flexible, and a quick learner. He is one of the few male managers who recognized, acknowledged, and encouraged my gifts. He worked hard to make sure I received the most out of my training and my time there.

Once again, financial concerns became an issue. When your parents teach you independence and you're stuck paying school loans, you find that even though you're doing better, it's still not enough. These are jobs, not careers. There's no financial security in them. And so I left Staples for a job that paid $4 an hour more.

It was the beginning of a downward trend that included losing my confidence and my business savvy. In 2016, I experienced a breakup that changed my life and the course of it. After living with this man for almost a year, he left me for another woman. I made the difficult decision to move home. I did not have the means to support myself.

There is a silver lining to this dark cloud, because it was during this time that I started on a personal journey to find myself again, and to explore what I truly desire out of life.

I decided to share my story and stop hiding behind the facade of pretending to be happy. I resumed my coaching journey and started *Command Your Confidence,* intending to teach women to find themselves and take them on a journey within to live as their true authentic self. I choose to lead by example and practice all I preach, so I committed to using my own tools and resources and continue to evolve.

Within months of starting on this journey, I was a self-proclaimed Master of Personal Evolution. My purpose, my branding, my programs, everything changed and focused on the message I have to share with women. I began to produce videos and share my journey and gained a nice following. And yet, not enough people wanted to buy my programs, or pay to learn about confidence.

The question became, "Do I keep going, so that one day I can be financially free, or should I stay in my nine to five?"

After twelve years in an endless cycle of retail and customer service jobs, I hit a breaking point. I realized I was not getting, and never would get, the most out of my capabilities in this field.

Then one day, a friend asked me to tell her about my gifts.

"I am awesome at writing and am a natural at communicating, speaking, and building relationships," I said. "I am creative and resourceful, an excellent strategist and planner, and am organized, efficient, results oriented, and great with time and talent management."

She summed up by saying, "So you're personable, have leadership skills, and like to express yourself. What else?"

I told her how I had always been a smart girl and how it got me into trouble. And in that moment, it was as if Pandora's box opened to me.

I said, "I'm intuitive and a big picture person and have amazing foresight. I can see issues, obstacles, and events coming before they happen. I'm able to think five steps ahead and even though I'm often only allowed to act two steps ahead. I'm a problem solver and because of that, I always have a plan A, B, and C. I'm innovative and can facilitate change, growth, expansion, and new ideas that will help in business and life."

Expressing these gifts gave light to the fact that for a long time, people and society have stuffed me into a little box when I was born to stand and be outside of it! And I let them do it!

Suddenly I understood. I chose to cast off the mantle I had put on as a hurt little girl trying to fit in. The massive personality and person that I am, came exploding through, allowing me to share, reveal, and step into my power for the first time in my life. I finally found the answer to who I am.

The Final Transformation: An Alpha Female of Business

I live and lead by the mantra of, "I was, I am, I will be." When I first drafted this story, I had ideas of how to use this chapter to leverage my journey as an entrepreneur. I thought that I would talk about my program of evolving entrepreneurs. I would talk about the hustle, and the struggle, and how for the longest time I had no clients even though people were following me, my story, and my journey. As I sat to write my chapter, I thought of both my personal story and my business story. I thought about my mantra:

I was, I am, I will be.

The release of my gifts is the 'I am' part of the mantra. When I rewrote my bio on my site after having the Pandora's box epiphany, I called myself, *The Alpha Female of Business*. This is who I always believed I am meant to be: A natural-born, intuitive leader who uses her gifts of foresight to protect those who don't yet have the courage or confidence to lead on their own.

When I think of an *Alpha Female*, wolves immediately spring to my mind's eye. There's a story called La Loba (the she-wolf). I'll give you the TLDR version (too long, didn't read). La Loba is the story of an old woman who lives in a hidden place that everyone knows of but where few have been. Those who come to her are lost or wandering people, they are seekers.

La Loba is known as the bone woman, and she collects and assembles the bones of skeletons. When she has a full skeleton she sings, and the bones turn to flesh. The flesh turns into a creature, and the creature becomes a wild woman who runs free toward the horizon. The La Loba story, if you think about it, describes the journey through one's soul and is an incredible story of transformation.

This is how I choose to lead, every single day. For me, a leader is not described by one, strict definition. A leader is someone who has the courage and confidence to evolve beyond that which society tells them they should be. A leader transforms, they are the innovators and change makers, and they are always ready and eager to evolve.

I was always a leader, I am a Master of Evolution and I will be the Alpha Female of Business.

AUTHOR MELISSA RODRIGUEZ

Originally a Master of Personal Evolution, Melissa has grown, transformed, and changed into a Master of Evolution, taking people on an incredible journey to go beyond society and self-imposed limitations. She has the gifts of intuition and foresight and knows how to use and leverage her gifts and skills to be a powerhouse businesswoman. Combining natural-born leadership skills with her passion for writing, speaking, and content creation allows Melissa's clients to go places within their souls that have been left in the dark all too long.

As an innovator and changemaker, Melissa facilitates change, growth, transformation, and of course, evolution.

About this writing, she says, "This chapter is dedicated to my family, and my sisters of Infinite Receiving, who support me in this wild, inspirational time of my life."

Connect with the Author. . .

Website: http://www.commandyourconfidence.com
Email: commandyourconfidence@gmail.com

"No one can achieve great success on their own. There need to be others who have gone before, and I follow in those footsteps, as well as create what I desire to do." ~ Annette Fluit

The Walk of Wonder

ANNETTE FLUIT

S andy has a hectic life. It was her choosing because of the impact she wants to make for her family and a specific set of people. However, the social online presence she developed into a business has led to success taking over her life! Moving to the new house created an unplanned break in her online connection, one Sandy at first found irritating, then as she spent more time reflecting and less reacting, she remembered how before the digital world, her life was simpler and quieter.

Sandy realized she was firmly headed in a direction; one in which her love of writing had been neglected far too long. She realized that God's creation was being squished out of her life as her walks and view of the natural was ebbing away. She also realized that her connection with nature is exactly where her imagination awakes and can be drawn upon.

As Sandy thought about what she had yet to accomplish today, she anticipated, with real pleasure, the walk she planned after all the unpacking and moving, even though her feet were swollen. She prayed for supernatural power to have all the energy supplied and it seemed endless!

Finally, at the end of the day she finished up the dishes, donned a light canvas colored dress that resembled a potato sack, and filled its small side pockets with a few necessities. Sandy felt instantly refreshed as she stepped onto the paved path behind their new home. The sun-dappled walkway presented greenery, a trickling stream, and various birds of a feather; sparrows, robins, cardinals and a few black birds. Her previous residence, although in view of a lake, proved to be dusty as the streets were busy. Construction crews were a constant in the year that they had lived there. She had missed this silence and the hush of the wind brushing through the trees.

Sandy paused on the meandering pathway (leading to the grocery store, her destination) to sit briefly on a wooden bench in the sun. In no mood to sit there and take on the sweltering heat, she resumed her walk, noting idly the strewn bread bits left for the birds to devour.

The quietness and the rustling of the trees was calming to her soul. No traffic, dust, or construction. Every now and again, the stream beckoned her to look, as it wandered alongside the human-packed earth just steps away. Willow trees of varying types grew along the water's edge. Homes were nestled on either side of this nature's hideaway and the walkway was clad with tall trees. You would never know that all around, people were living. No shouts of children, no lawnmowers; just quiet.

In the shade, off to the left and at the intersection of the main street, Sandy saw that her favorite bench was empty! She had been walking long enough to welcome a break and flopped onto the black steel park bench. She lifted her tired, aching legs and feet to stretch out on the length of the bench. She closed her eyes, listening to bees buzz among the tall grass. Birds continued to make their presence known, flying to and fro, their wings singing as the air lifted them from the tree branches. The trickling music of the stream in the background blended into a symphony that proved to calm Sandy's soul.

"How did I let this go?" Sandy spoke quietly, the question addressed to herself.

She opened her eyes and for several minutes, enjoyed the scene. Beneath the earth was teaming with life, the grasses also talking in their own way, the bees gathered in harmony to talk with the grasses. It seemed natural for each party to make their way into this haven of oneness. Off to the right, a monarch butterfly made its way into view, fluttering and challenging the scene with its beauty. It had no care but to use its surroundings as part of its habitat.

Just beside this wonderful bit of forest, new homes were going up to make yet another subdivision. It seemed that the world was getting busier by the day and Sandy, knowing that the presence of the forest is what drew her to this place, hoped the new homes did not change the calm she found here. Each subdivision had its own communication style; each community nestled in its own accord to make one major community.

As her thoughts turned to her life, she used this time to conjure her imagination and sense what the presence and communication of the forest had to do with leadership. Up until eight months previously, Sandy had experienced what most people do when they open a business or proudly display their excitement about a particular area of interest. It was all up front! "See, see, see!" was the motto. "Buy, buy, buy!", was another mantra. It didn't matter whether an audience or an individual were looking. "Take, take, take! Sample, sample, sample! Tell, tell, tell!" All the words, all of her words, were about making the sale. In the online space, it can even be worse. Everyone wants you to know what they are doing and want you to participate!

In the forest, Sandy's eyes were opened. The forest doesn't have words; it doesn't say anything. It is there; to be viewed, admired, stepped into. Sandy was beckoned because of its presence, its beauty and character. It neither flaunted nor proclaimed all that it represented. When Sandy stepped into the forest's world, she threw away her email address.

Of course, humans are much different from a forest. Their mouths speak their thoughts. And sometimes, they question, although it seems most people don't know what it's like to lead with questions. In comparison, the forest asks no questions. You may ask questions of it. What questions are you asking? What kind are you asking?

Remember when you were in school? The questions began with who, what, where, how, and sometimes why. What happened to those questions? Why are we not asking them? School begins in the home. Telling. That's what Sandy experienced. Tell me this, you should do this, do that. In the collaborated school, the opposite is true. "Ask questions," the teacher remarks.

The only school of thought that Sandy knew was in the home. It took three long years for her to know what kind of questions to ask.

Sandy now understands what it is to be a leader. It is to be and to beckon, to attract because of the kind of person she is. The epiphany Sandy has on this day is that she loves being a leader, but doesn't like how her own leadership skills took her away from her creative side. In her little piece of forest, she came to understand that she had time to make amends and turn her life around.

The big word for Sandy is trust. Trust in the God she serves and the gifts and talents she already has inside of her. She is determined to use what was already ignited in her; her strength is in her creative side, in words, in objects to behold!

Was it a weakness to work on things she wasn't good at? No, for that too is part of the journey. Sandy will go forward to be a communicator like the forest. She will be a communicated leader who knows how to ask the finer questions, to pull the answers out of her audience.

Sandy is meeting a new success challenge! She is becoming the listener. The true leader is one who knows how to ask questions and listen to the speaker, just as the forest spoke to Sandy. Sandy chooses to draw people to her, just as the forest draws people to it.

She is sharing her leadership. She is stepping out of the forest, always to return, to show the world her light, to share her presence, and listen to the hearts and desires of her audience.

Words are important to Sandy. She so desired to be the opposite of what she had been known for; loud and boisterous and all up front, that she chose a new direction. She wants to be molded into the opposite of what she was and has accepted the challenge of leadership.

Her path stretches before her and it is lifelong; learning, studying and implementing. Her work is to have relationships in the way of friendship and to draw people to toward her; not because of what others could do for her but because of the presence she is and what she does and what she led others to do.

Be like the forest. Be a presence and communicate a style so others want to step into your world because you stepped into theirs.

AUTHOR ANNETTE FLUIT

"Great leaders always seem to embody two seemingly disparate qualities. They are both highly visionary and highly practical." ~ John C. Maxwell

To Annette, leadership is an ongoing journey, one on which she continues to evolve and grow, changing as challenges are met and resolved. She sees situations and people like diamonds whose words, thoughts, and actions are powerful enough to impact another life. Annette believes in the importance of vision to leadership, both having clarity and passion in seeing the vision and the skills to enable others to understand and embrace it.

It was when Annette entered the network marketing industry that her inner journey turned toward providing leadership to others. Meeting incredible leaders and learning how to run a business with no experience, Annette understood that old patterns and behaviors can be changed by renewing the mind and applying new ones.

"In the past three years, I have gone through personal challenges when it comes to communication. I thought I was a great communicator, and it came as a shock to realize the opposite. I overpowered the conversation, had excellent eye contact but truly didn't listen to people's issues and problems. I didn't have the patience to listen.

What I have discovered through the network marketing industry is that leadership is much more than selling and influencing people to buy. It's quite different. Understanding, learning, and repeatedly applying new skills takes a new thought pattern. I have discovered what it truly means to be a person of attraction and to create the type of life I want to lead. I won't ever go back to my initial way of doing things."

Annette believes in the importance of moving through fear to achieve greatness. She relates a time when, as a young girl, she rode her first bicycle.

"It had a light blue frame, shiny handle bars, and a well-used black seat. I took it to the back road to give it a go. Intentionally, I shook the handle bars, as my older brother instructed. The bike began to shake uncontrollably, and I had to hang on for dear life so as not to fall off! The gravel road and the bike frame were having a party and clearly it was time to steady those handle bars. Eventually, the ride steadied. And then, I shook those bars again. I liked that shake, rattle and roll experience! It was risky and great!"

Annette believes that the mark of a true leader is having the strength to authentically look within themselves and make the discoveries that will enable change. She is dedicated to reviving and teaching the art of communication. Like throwing a stone to skip in the water, small changes spread out to cause ripples with broader effect.

Connect with the Author. . .

Website: http://www.annettefluit.com/
Social Media
  Facebook: https://www.facebook.com/annette.fluit
  Facebook: https://www.facebook.com/groups/415181962181938/
  Instagram: https://www.instagram.com/fluitannette/
Email: annette.t.fluit@gmail.com

"Leadership is the ability to create success so that everyone rises together." ~ *Becky Stonebarger*

The Glass Slipper Story: A Transformational Experience

BECKY STONEBARGER

I have always had a princess fantasy and firmly believe that there is nothing I cannot do in the world. My first awareness that I have a unique take on leadership and how this has woven through my life came the day I purchased a box of small glass slippers from a thrift store. As I pulled them out of the box, marveling at the tender care taken to wrap each with beautiful ribbon, I didn't even know what compelled me to buy them, but I had a vision that one day they would be used.

Leadership is the ability to see other people falling and have the courage to lift them up.

I remember talking about my feelings when I was told I had six months to live. My answer was direct. I recall saying, "I want to keep living." Pretty simple, huh? There was no room in my mind to believe that I would be beaten by cancer. I would not accept any belief that I would not make it in life.

I survived cancer by making shifts in my thinking and beliefs. When I got the diagnosis that I had the Big C, I was devastated. My first bout with cancer happened before I became self-employed and I didn't want anyone to know. And yet something within me, almost at once, told me that I was destined to beat it so I could help others see their own power to thrive. I had big dreams and intended to reach them all, fighting for each and every one. The princess mindset that served me well from childhood to adulthood refused to give up.

My Childhood Business Mindset

I started my entrepreneurial journey as a child. My mother was single and money was scarce. Giving and getting gifts was something that didn't exist for us. I remember one May when I wanted to buy my mom presents because it was Mother's Day and her birthday month.

It was obvious to me that I would have to get creative about how to finance these presents. I dug nickels out of the couch cushions and put them into a bubble gum machine to get prizes. Then I created a carnival in my back yard. The neighborhood kids paid to come to the backyard carnival to win the prizes. I sold popcorn and apples we picked off the neighbor's trees. When my brothers and I were given marionette puppets, I expanded the business by bringing my brothers in as partners, and built an entire theatre to put on both the backyard carnival and a puppet show.

I was the usher inside, selling tickets. To discover that people pay for entertainment formed a fun foundation that's led me to where I am today. I always felt that I was a princess, and this was the time when I knew that I was the princess in charge of my life, and the leader of my world. I discovered that people pay money for unusual things! Especially when collaboration and leadership was involved, and there was a good sales presentation to accompany it.

Once the light of an entrepreneur fire is lit, it keeps on shining and changing.

Because I was the youngest child of a single mother, my role model was my grandfather, who was a business man. I watched everything he did and learned his style. I always had my own style as well, and I knew that one day, my perfectly sized glass slipper would find me.

When my mom remarried an insurance man, I had a second role model who happened to also be a business person. Ironically, my love of networking began by watching my mom and new-father go to dances. It was from the dances that most of his business leads were generated. I eventually started to work my way up in the family business and learn more about networking and collaboration.

Cancer Cured Me...

My Glass Slipper Story is that I never once believed cancer would take my life. Rather, I continued on my journey as if it never existed.

In the early days after my diagnosis, I was deeply in the Feel Sorry for Myself mode. The more time I spent wallowing in pity, the worse my symptoms got. I became overweight and lazy. And in retrospect, I should not have been surprised that, after being cleared of the first cancer, I developed a second variant. Then, while in treatment for the second cancer, the first returned! I found myself in a position where I had to do something, and fast.

I woke up one day and decided that I didn't want people to feel sorry for me and I didn't want to feel sorry for myself either. I researched the type of cancer I had and determined that its cause did not stem from abusing my body, or from anything I had done. I stopped beating myself up over this diagnosis and decided that I wanted to live. It was at that moment that I turned my thoughts toward living. I have survived three bouts with two different cancers!

"You Have Six Months to Live." When the doctor said this to me, it had a profound effect. His words, this exact sentence, is what motivated me to live. Remembering this deadline (in the truest sense of the word), motivated me to lose over 100 pounds of weight. It motivated me to ensure that I created something for my husband to tuck away if something happened to me.

My Glass Slipper Kept Appearing

My secret to surviving was that very few people knew about the cancer. The second cancer was a carcinoma that showed up on my face, and there was no denying it was there. By not talking about it, not feeding it with fear of dying, and walking past the diagnosis with my head high and my mindset clear. I believe I kicked it through thought.

The Slipper and I finally met...

During the years I was battling cancer, I continued to learn how to lead myself and be the creator of my own life. The more positive and forward moving I was, the closer my glass slipper came. It felt good.

I was making choices that were positive and focused on the future. It was a conscious choice to center my world on the outcome I wanted to see, and expected to see, rather than on what I was being told was my fate. I continued to focus on growing and developing my business and making new connections. The connections were positive, and they helped me heal my life. I only remember two of the 30 radiation treatments. The treatments were the fuel to the fire of my business.

The glass slipper was waiting for me, and I wanted to meet it. Being diagnosed with cancer empowered me to truly focus on the life I wanted to live. It showed me that I had to love myself first and to create the dream life I desired.

One month after the doctor's original six-month prediction expired, I went for blood work and found the cancer in remission! It remains in remission to this day! I did the work, I held the belief that I would be a successful business owner, and I would not be a victim. There are miracles in the glass slipper story.

I placed my tiny, cancer free, healed-by-Grace foot into the Glass Slipper and exploded the glass ceiling mindset surrounding cancer. You can do it too. Just keep your mind on the positive, whether it's a glass slipper, or a new love. It's all up to you.

Teaching Points.

Life can beat us down, scare us to death and make us lose hope. However, when you turn your thoughts and full attention to what you want rather than allowing what you don't want to cloud your vision, you are on your way to realizing your own glass slipper story. There is only one slipper for you, and it's waiting for you now.

1. Be positive and walk toward your ideal experience.
2. Don't let your thoughts go to victim mode. If they start going there, say that you are the princess of your own experience.
3. Create a tribe, and love them hard, and expect them to love you back.
4. Believe that your body is a healing machine and wants to give you balance in life.
5. Maintain a know, like, and trust platform which you can borrow for your own growth.

Today I run two successful business and I feel more beautiful and sexy than ever. I have incorporated mastermind meetings into my business model and have grown beyond local connections to include national and international collaborations.

That box of glass slippers? The beautiful trinkets have turned into reminders for me. I am reminded of my journey each time I see one of those delicate slippers and am reminded of all those I've helped, and all those who are yet to come into my life.

AUTHOR BECKY STONEBARGER

Once upon a time, there was a young girl who wanted to be a Princess. Today she is the owner of multiple businesses, a survivor of cancer, and dedicated to teaching young girls and women how to fight for what they want, even in the face of unsurmountable odds. Her core value system focuses on developing and sustaining the Know, Like, and Trust platform.

Becky Stonebarger has a passion for connecting people and making them more successful. Prior to founding Business Connections of Nevada, direct sales entrepreneurship had been Becky's career path for nearly three decades. Through the years she has marketed everything from scrapbooks to personal security products. The constant in her career is her fervent attention to planning and details and a commitment to providing her clients with outstanding customer service.

Becky started her first business when she was a child; carnivals and puppet theaters for children in her neighborhood. She excelled at team building even then and attributes much of her success as a businessperson to her ability to harness the talents of others through collaborative efforts.

Becky has also held prominent leadership roles in a host of non-profit organizations. She started Girl Scout troops and youth ministries across the country and received recognition and awards as a leader. In addition, she has held volunteer leadership positions in Eastern Star, Job's Daughters, and Angel Tree. Introducing children to community service brings her the most happiness and fulfillment.

With friends all over the United States, Becky's name often comes up in conversation between people who meet for the first time, and nurturing lasting relationships has always been important to Becky. Her 31-year marriage to husband Gil, is one of her proudest achievements. She also has two beautiful daughters and two lovely grandchildren.

As the CEO of Business Connections of Nevada, Becky is pursuing her lifelong purpose by helping entrepreneurs connect and build effective relationships. Her organization nurtures small to medium sized businesses through weekly connection meetings, and by offering The Beacon Center, a 1,300-square foot meeting facility, for rent at an affordable rate. Becky Stonebarger is a woman of influence who envisions the success of others and helps them to achieve their goals.

Connect with the Author. . .

Website: http:// www.beckystonebarger.com
Social Media
  Author Page: http://amazon.com/author/beckystonebarger
  LinkedIn: https://www.linkedin.com/in/beckystonebarger
  Facebook: https://www.facebook.com/becky.stonebarger

"As a leader, you must do more than pretend to care. Put in the effort. Build real, genuine, deep, and lasting relationships with others." ~ *Lea Durbin*

Walking a Path Less Travelled

LEA DURBIN

*E*veryone has a story that begs to be told. Like everyone who walks this earth today, I have many, ranging from happy to sad, triumph to tragedy. Over the years, I've learned it's in the stories that we can learn the simplest and yet most profound leadership lessons.

When faced with a life altering journey, taking the easy road can be an almost automatic response to the situation. We all know people who make themselves the victim by taking a woe is me path or look for sympathy, and many times pity, from others. I don't believe in that type of thinking.

After dinner on Thanksgiving, 2013 our daughter Rachel, calmly told us that she had found a lump a few days before. I was not as calm as we spent a week waiting anxiously for the biopsy result, praying it would be negative. On December 2, 2013, we received the words no one wants to hear: At 31-years-old, my daughter had invasive ductal carcinoma, breast cancer.

Rachel was confident that everything would be fine and that her course of treatment would cure her. She underwent chemotherapy, bilateral mastectomy, and reconstruction. Throughout her treatment she never wavered in her determination to beat this horrific disease. In early February 2015, she was considered in full remission.

In March 2016, I received a call that rocked my world. After a trip to the ER for what seemed like appendicitis, we were informed that her cancer had metastasized to her liver.

I immediately went into she's going to fight and survive mode. The first time around was only the preparation for what we would face. After the medical workups and treatment plans were discussed, she chose to begin an aggressive treatment program. She had a reaction to the chemotherapy and almost died with the first session. Two weeks later, we were preparing to say our final goodbye. And she rallied back! I remember her looking at me and saying, "I promised you I would fight this and I am."

Those words still haunt me.... It's my job to fix the hurts and make things better. But I couldn't fix this for her.

My days blurred together that spring as we traversed a new and different journey together. All my time and energy was focused on helping her fight this awful disease, in whatever capacity she needed from me. Unbeknownst to many, even when she was fighting for her own life, she was providing support and help to families with chronic illness. She refused to give up and continued to find ways to stay busy and productive.

I never let myself think about where we could end up. If I had, I would not have been able to keep going. I simply did whatever needed to be done in that moment. I dealt with her illness by focusing on my work of helping others while I helped her. I needed to know in my heart of hearts that while taking care of her, I was also taking steps to keep her legacy alive.

Over the next three months, the roller coaster ride continued. We faced life threatening complications and hospitalizations that almost took her from us. We overcome them and healed well enough to go home, only to dip down into an emergency again and climb back up to encouraging stability.

I can't pinpoint when it happened, but my tolerance for insensitivity to patient rights by caregivers grew thin. My perspective changed. I watched as her voice was lost among all the medical discussions and decisions that were made. I worked to ensure that even if it appeared she wasn't comprehending or taking part in the discussions, her voice and wishes were heard and followed. Once again, I found myself alone, walking a path others couldn't begin to understand.

Supportive colleagues and friends constantly asked, "Where do you find the strength? I don't know how you're doing it."

My answer was easy, I prayed and relied on God and Jesus to get us through this.

In late June. a simple cold was the beginning of the end. Rachel was in constant pain, yet she always smiled, and always had a kind word for everyone. She showed signs that she was tired; she ate less, slept more, the sparkle in her eyes faded, and the tone of her voice softened. Others either didn't notice or simply overlooked the signs, but I was keenly aware. Every moment became the most important moment with her. We both were learning what true strength meant: Rachel for being strong in her fight to survive and me to finally understand what *Thy Will* really means.

We prayed relentlessly from the beginning for her healing. It was during one of my prayers toward the end that provided me with a revelation. God's Will would allow her to heal—in Heaven. On Sunday, July 10, she woke up, asked for something to eat, and a glass of water. Within a few hours, she whispered, "I'm really tired of fighting."

I leaned in, kissed her and told her it was ok and she could stop. I told her I would always love her.

She responded, "I love you more." Within an hour, she was gone and the world I had known was forever changed.

In the months following her passing, as I rebuilt my life and struggled to move forward, I had little tolerance for superficial conversations and interactions. Genuine, sincere, and real interactions mattered. Honesty and trust became a critical value in my relationships. The hardest lesson I learned is that many will walk away. Some because you're dealing with something they can't understand, others because they fear your grief will rub off on them.

Over my 25-year career I often found myself on a path alone. Being alone this time was different.

It never gets easier, but you learn how to deal with it.

I don't consider myself a leader. I simply do what needs to be done to help others, or make a difference in the lives of those who are struggling, in an authentic and genuine manner. I don't care about titles or climbing a ladder. Ever since I was a little girl, I've been told I'm overly sensitive, that I think differently, I process information differently, I take things too personally, and feel things on a much deeper level than my friends and colleagues. After the loss of my daughter, this tendency in myself became more pronounced and I am now much more aware in every interaction that occurs.

Being fully present and aware in every interaction allows me to listen more closely and hear what wasn't being said. I put away my cell phone, laptop, or tablet and focus only on the person and people in front of me. This results in deeper conversations that allow true collaboration and problem solving to occur.

When you are driven to help others, this type of awareness is critical to ensure that their voices are heard. This isn't a revelation by any means. But it is slowly being replaced by the instant responses that are becoming more accepted. When you put others first, the value you place on them is evident and the relationship deepens naturally.

All relationships are built on trust. You must put in the effort to make them last. You need a level of authenticity, sincerity, and genuine interest that goes beyond the superficial and small talk. Create an environment where you can speak freely and openly. This can take time, but the result is a deep, meaningful, and lasting relationship.

Being different and walking a path less traveled is where I find peace and gain my future direction. It's okay to walk alone.

I don't work toward goals and achievements for anyone but myself. The recognition I've received in my career was a complete surprise and came about when others noticed my efforts and results, not because I sought attention. There are good reasons to celebrate your achievements with others, but my most meaningful recognition has occurred without others. It was simply given by those who acknowledged me. I was able to cherish the moment, in the moment.

If you find yourself at a crossroads, or on a path you weren't expecting. Stop and take a moment to breathe. Think about your journey and allow yourself to feel the feelings. Listen to your heart—it won't let you down.

AUTHOR LEA DURBIN

Lea Durbin is a Dreamer, People Connector, an Advocate for those less fortunate, and Catalyst for Change. She's driven to help others reach higher and achieve their goals by building them up and walking alongside them every step of the way. She uses her passion to engage individuals, teams, organizations and communities in a meaningful manner while empowering them to make a lasting difference with a far-reaching and deep impact.

Lea is an avid Drag Racing Fan and taking a race car down the track at over 200 mph is on her bucket list! She lives with her husband and two dogs in Bainbridge, Indiana and can be found at:

Connect with the Author. . .

Website: www.facebook.com/lea.durbin
Social Media
  Twitter: https://twitter.com/LeaDurbin
  Instagram: www.instagram.com/connectstohelp
  LinkedIn: www.linkedin.com/in/leadurbin

"If you are dissatisfied with any aspect of your life, the good news is you can change it, no matter your age circumstances or education....NO excuses. It can be done." ~ Dorothy Neddermeyer

Are You a Collaborative Leader?

LEADING YOUR FAMILY, BUSINESS, OR COMPANY

DOROTHY M. NEDDERMEYER

Collaboration in life and business has been heralded as a sign of an effective, high-functioning person and organization.

In families, collaboration means that everyone understands and accepts the common focus and goals. Each person, including children as they are able, is willing to do their part effectively and as needed.

In many large organizations achieving collaboration means breaking down cubicles and office walls and guiding employees to work together—Apple and Google are two examples of collaborative work environments. Although, this approach worked for many employees, others have been unenthusiastic. As a Collaborative family or business leader, choosing to embrace collaboration is an investment strategy.

The decision to develop a collaborative approach with the family and employees begins with deciding what collaboration benefits your family or organization needs. Here are seven of the most used and likely most effective benefit of collaboration:

1. *Collaboration moves a family, team, or company more effectively towards its goals.*

A Work.com study revealed that 97 percent of Collaborative Leaders, employees, and executives agreed that the level of collaboration directly impacts the outcome of a task or project and on the bottom line. When a team or department collaborate effectively, openly sharing information and able to communicate seamlessly, they can work at their most effective level.

On the other hand, when Affiliate, Associates, Teams, and Employees work solo, it can take longer to reach their goals. As the Work.com study revealed, the most effective balance is individual focus with team collaboration. Not every person does their best when they are constantly in close contact with others; many need alone time balanced with teamwork. Collaboration technology, such as video conferencing and desktop sharing, enables this balance because it seamlessly links end users when collaboration makes sense—rather than all day, every day.

2. *Collaboration creates greater flexibility and support.*

Today's collaborative technology, such as cell phones, iPads, and Smartphones, enables people to work more flexibly than they might in the traditional nine-to-five office day. Many Multi-Level Marketing (MLM) associates and leaders can work on the road and even take advantage of real-time collaborative capabilities with remote associates around the globe. This level of flexibility fits many people's lifestyles better than a strict number of hours for a workday. And improved flexibility can lead to greater efficiency and effectiveness. A 16-year study by Idea Champions revealed that only three percent of people come up with their best ideas at work. The other 97 percent said they discover great ideas daily, at home, on vacation, and even in the shower. These anecdotes are in line with the Law of Attraction. With the mobile capabilities of collaboration technology, people can take advantage of sudden bursts of creativity and productivity—rather than confine themselves to rigid time frames.

3.   *Collaboration appeals to the tech-savvy.*

In many industries, younger and tech-savvy people are more likely to gravitate toward collaboration technology, since technology is such a large part of their life already. Millennials are especially supportive of collaboration to improve productivity; one study revealed that 49 percent of Millennials support social tools, such as Skype, Google Hangout, Zoom and Face-time, for collaboration on an as needed basis or regular get-togethers.

Many Millennials are moving into businesses. They look for team leader, supervisor, and manager level positions. Now is the time for C-Suite executives, employers, and organizations to foster a collaborative environment. I notice Millennials are posting on Social Media about products they sell through direct sales companies. For example: ASEA, cubicles, Chloe and Isabel, Stella and Dot, Rodan + Fields and Pampered Chef are a few of the more popular LWM businesses.

Older businesses such as Avon, Mary Kay, Melaleuca, and Amway are more attractive to the Silent and Baby Boomer generations. (Read more at: https://www.moneyunder30.com/multi-level-marketing-side-hustle .) It is interesting to note that 20 percent of U.S. millionaires own a business. Collaboration at its best.

4.   *Collaboration engages remote and work-from-home businesses and employees.*

Despite the benefits of working remotely, sometimes it can leave people feeling cut off from coworkers or their peers. By fostering a high level of collaboration, major company ensures that all employees—whether they work from home, headquarters or an overseas office—benefit from real-time information and continual communication. This higher level of engagement means that an organization or company will also benefit from the knowledge and expertise of all Associates/employees, no matter their location.

5. *Collaboration assists new employees to get up to speed.*

New employees or Associates learn best from their colleagues and higher-ups and learning is best achieved through collaboration. In addition, collaboration creates a natural mentor-mentee relationship between new employees or Associates and their veteran counterparts, which helps inspire and engage both groups even more.

What benefits of collaboration in the workplace have you seen in your career? How have you seen today's technology enable a higher level of collaboration?

In the family, collaboration fosters an atmosphere of inclusion and involvement. Children as young as two-years-old can learn easy tasks. For example, my two-year-old daughter packed her luggage without telling me. I waited until she was asleep before I investigated her luggage. And to my utter surprise she had packed everything she needed! (Except, not enough panties I am sure she didn't count the days.) Older sibs can engage with younger sibs as mentors and both teach and learn leadership skills within the family.

6. *Collaboration among family members and between businesses.*

Collaboration, between parents and children, grandparents, aunts, uncles, cousins, friends, and neighbors enriches everyone's learning experience. Collaboration between businesses is the process of pooling knowledge, resources and relationships for the sake of achieving shared aims. It is a delicate balance to be sure.

Collaboration with vendors is age-old. The competitive nature of getting the best price or receiving the best price often engenders a power struggle versus collaboration. Yet, when approached with a win/win attitude, everyone will win.

Collaboration expands the toolbox that a family or business has to flourish and build a strong foundation of prosperity. Openly sharing information requires trust and integrity. It is best to develop a strong collaborative relationship between family members, like-minded company cultures, individual contributors, and individual values.

7. Collaboration is the key to a family and organization's success

CEOs and human resources professionals agree collaboration increases employee and Associate management skills, cohesiveness, and productivity. Collaborative leadership creates higher profitability and is the key to an organization's success.

In view of these benefits, does it make sense to use the collaborative creativity of family members, employees, and Associates and include external stakeholders to generate those much-needed breakthrough ideas and ensure strong leadership?

Recently, I talked with an ASEA Associate who said one of her associates didn't like working with her. I suggested that maybe she could switch with an Associate within her group—it was a successful switch and both parties are happy with the change. This is collaborative leadership at its best.

Given the right circumstances, a collaborative idea combined with a management system of tools and practices, will help you carry out collaborative initiatives. Lead by example. Tap into innovation energy from employees, partners, Associates, and customers. Be a collaborative leader. It will improve your ability to respond to what emerges, find differentiating opportunities, drive a culture of collaboration and innovation, and create a simpatico that validates everyone's contribution as important for the future of your business or organization.

AUTHOR DOROTHY M. NEDDERMEYER, PHD

As a leading-edge Executive, Business and Personal Health consultant, conference keynote speaker with international experience, CEO/Founder, Dorothy M. Neddermeyer, Ph.D. provides company-wide business and personal improvement initiatives to optimize all resources to deliver strategic advantage with measurable outcomes.

In 30+ years of experience, Dr. Dorothy has mentored executives, couples, families, and entrepreneurs worldwide to experience their highest potential through powerful Eastern/Western strategic tools and leading-edge focus on Cultural factors, discovering and resolving mental blocks, fears and self-hindering beliefs.

Connect with the Author. . .

Website: http://drdorothy.info/
Social Media
  Facebook: https://www.facebook.com/DrDorothyNed
  LinkedIn: https://www.linkedin.com/in/dorothymneddermeyer/
  Twitter: https://twitter.com/dorothyned

"You are designed to lead a life of purpose, pursue it with clarity, and give back so others may follow." ~ *Laraine Sacco*

Succeed Through Confidence to Living The Dream

LARAINE SACCO

What do you do when you know deep down in your soul that you are designed to be a blessing to others? Do you believe in yourself? Was there ever a time in your life when you did something because you felt deep down you were supposed to do it? You have leadership qualities within you and may already be a Leader in your business or you wouldn't be reading this book.

Destined to be a Leader

Before I believed in me I believed in others. Many who know me are surprised to hear that I was incredibly shy, overweight, had a speech impediment, and was afraid. My life was filled with hurt and even within my heart I always felt I didn't belong.

Why was I being punished?

Speaking was a painful process. Every time I spoke there was correction. It made me want to just stay quiet. If I could say the sounds correctly, the teacher and my parents would bribe me with cookies. In my head, it always sounded the way it was supposed to sound however it didn't materialize verbally.

I grew up feeling *less than* for so many reasons. How did I become a Global Recruiter and Success Coach against all odds? How is it that I now get to work when I want, where I want, with who I want and live the life I've always dreamed? You can have this, too!

The First Success Can Begin at a Young Age

My first memory of being successful was selling, promoting, and sharing Girl Scout cookies with every homeowner within a mile. I can still remember the happy smiles of every person who opened the door once they saw the cookies!

The excitement of sharing my happiness revolved around cookies and I knew how each one tasted and how it made me feel. I was number one in sales in the history of my troop at the age of five!

And yet even in triumph, the trophy and acknowledgement made me feel uncomfortable. There were girls who felt I didn't deserve it. This created so much conflict within my mind.

I loved making people happy which is why I just kept going door to door. I didn't understand jealousy! A few years later I won an art contest. My best friend stood up and yelled I didn't deserve the award! Betrayal once again and it tasted bad!

Create the person you know is inside you

Growing up in a world where I never felt I belonged, there were people telling me to be different, tougher, meaner, thick skinned. I felt I was not valued and was told I was too sensitive. This life made me question everything about myself. Can you relate?

As I grew up, I knew there was a better way, but the negative reactions of those who *loved* me always led me down a different path.

What changed? I did. If you don't change your thoughts, your actions will remain the same. Surround yourself with people who will lift you up to achieve your goals. Listen to podcasts, read books, stay motivated, have an accountability partner, share your dream, share your journey.

How does it happen? Take risks. In my teens, I began a business because I knew I could help people as an entrepreneur. I listened to what they needed and provided an option. At a young age, I started a 'cookie' company and had 32 types of cookies. I charged more money than the bakery and still was successful. The biggest mistake I made was I only had one oven.

Another time I asked for a lot more money when interviewing for a traditional job and stood my ground. The Vice President asked, "Why should we pay you that much money?"

My response, "Because I'm worth it." I was absolutely terrified because at that time I was running out of money and didn't have any job options. I took a big risk, but I got the job and the money I wanted!

Why are experiences important?

Every experience, thought, and person who came into my life happened for a reason. You are here for a purpose! Whatever I have done in my life you can do it too! Becoming a Leader didn't happen overnight, but I do believe I was Conceived to Lead. And so are you!

What is Leadership?

Leadership is defined as someone who helps people achieve things they don't think are possible. Leaders are coaches with a passion for developing people and translate a vision into reality.

Leadership is about giving people the tools they need to succeed by encouraging openness, authenticity and positive influence. To be a Leader, you want to focus on clarity, confidence, and being courageous. You want to step out of your comfort zone. Each time you do something scary, like posting a face book live video or speaking in front of others, you develop your skills. Become a problem solver. Help others achieve their goals and build the next generation of leaders. Listening is key! Become an active and engaged listener. Embrace FEAR: Forget Everything and Run toward your dream!

What is Your Vision?

It's time to be crystal clear as to your goals. Start by writing them as quickly as you can. Then go back and focus on each goal. Is it fitness, health, financial? Create realistic goals and stretch goals.

A goal without a plan is just a wish, a goal without a plan is planning to fail. You have your goals written. Now design your perfect day. It's called Visualizations. This is different from a vision board. The vision board encompasses what you want with your money: the perfect house, your mountain home, your expensive car or trips. To achieve the income to make your vision come true you need to visualize— what your actions are; what you need to achieve—on a daily basis.

Failing to Plan is Planning to Fail. Do you know who originally said this? Benjamin Franklin. He is also the Father of Time Management! Control your calendar to 15-minute intervals to accomplish more.

Qualities that make a Great Leader

Be an honest, authentic, and ethical Leader who communicates your vision. Delegate others and help them to step into their Leadership role. Be accountable and commit to your team. Be a role model and guide for your team. Inspire others to feel and be successful and to see the vision. Good Leaders inspire confidence to handle all situations in a calm, positive manner.

Leadership develops over time. I would love to hear about your leadership story. It is my honor to meet you and be part of your journey to living the dream because you are *Conceived to Lead.*

AUTHOR LARAINE SACCO

Laraine Sacco is a Global Recruiter and Success Coach, Author, Speaker, Wife and Mom who believes in God, family and helping others to achieve their greatness!

Laraine is a co-author in three International Best-Selling Books, The Missing Piece in Business, The Missing Piece in Forgiveness, and Chocolate & Diamonds for the Woman's Soul.

Conceived to Lead is her fourth compilation and in it she tells the story of a young girl who knew she was to lead others in finding their path to success with tips for success. Her fifth book *Letters to My Father*, compiled by Tammy Jurnett-Lewis, launches in December 2017

Join Laraine in her next successful book *Stepping Stones—Creating Pathways to Living The Dream*. Take your life and business to the next level by contacting Laraine today to continue your journey with confidence to *Living The Dream*

Connect with the Author. . .

Feel free to visit my website, www.LaraineSacco.com to learn more about how I became a Global Recruiter, Success Coach and International Author. Schedule a 15-minute appointment with no obligation to receive free advice and a plan of action.

Website: www.LaraineSacco.com
Social Media
  Facebook: https://www.facebook.com/laraine.sacco
  LinkedIn: https://www.linkedin.com/larainsacco
  Twitter: https://twitter.com/Laraine_Sacco
  Instagram: https://www.instagram.com/laraine.sacco

"Leadership is finding your own truth, honouring it, and supporting others to do the same." ~ *Claire Ryan Heatley*

My Journey Back to Me

CLAIRE RYAN HEATLEY

I was in my mid 30s when it finally hit me. It wasn't a dramatic wallop, but more of a gentle slap.

The Big Slap had come a couple years earlier. I suffered with one irritating, troublesome illness and injury after another. Exhausted to the point where I physically couldn't get out of bed, my body struggled to get my attention but I didn't get it.

You see my take on things at the time was this—a few days in bed, a large dose of vitamin C, some restful sleep, and I would be back to normal. In reality, days turned into weeks while I struggled to lift my head from the pillow. Even a toilet trip was a tremendous effort. The weeks turned into months, filled with much searching and frustration, and eventually a diagnosis of Myalgic Encephalopathy Chronic Fatigue Syndrome (ME/CFS).

The joy I felt thinking that I had answers and the hope of a quick fix turned into despair when I realized this was a chronic debilitating illness, with no proven cure or even any real treatment options. I set about educating myself and what I found was bleak. Talk of stalling lives, unable to work, wheelchairs, housebound, debates about its true origin, and lack of consensus on whether it even existed.

I, for one can tell you—it did exist, large and looming in my and my family's life. In my experience, the condition is real indeed. I find it to be incredulous that there are medics who still believe it is, "Not even a real disease." I can also tell you there is hope of a return to health. It took me five years of searching, experimenting with different treatments and therapies but slowly, over time my health returned. During the worst periods, it seemed like every system in my body was affected. I had gone, almost overnight it seemed from being active to nearly an invalid. The journey back to health was a much slower process and at times I felt like giving up. Through it all I had a committed determination that I would one day recover and I did.

I had always had tremendously tight neck and shoulders. I often had problems with backache and sciatica. No wonder—given I felt the weight of responsibility for the world and its wounded was on my shoulders. Constant demands of being a mum and working full time, mostly night shifts, began to take its toll. My Irritable Bowel Syndrome, and food sensitivities increased (an indication that there may be an issue with honoring one's boundaries and nourishing one's self). I had asthma, sinusitis, chronic rhinitis, migraines, and repeated strains, sprains and injuries.

These were the whispers from my body trying to get my attention. I was completely out of alignment. The imbalances and misalignments remained unchecked and became more extreme over time. My body had little choice but to scream loudly at me. Hence the Big Slap in the form of my illness.

Before ME/CFS, my days were full. I worked full time, enjoyed a busy life as a mum to two young girls and step mum to three older children, was social, active, involved in a local charity, and attended fast paced Zumba classes. I was intelligent and articulate with a real zest for life. I was a person whose motto was *life is for living and there is always a solution*. My life was an adventure and things were good.

Suddenly everything changed. I felt like I'd been run over by a bus. I struggled to remember my daughters' names, talking, thinking even, was exhausting and nobody could give me any answers.

My family was baffled as I was. I looked the same. On the outside nothing changed. It appeared that I was only bit tired. In truth my body felt battered and broken, struggling just to be.

What is Normal?

What I'd never realized was how excessive my *normal* was. People often commented on my lifestyle saying, "You're always busy.", "Do you ever sit down?", "How do you keep going?", and "You get more done in 24 hours than I can do in a week."

Did it ring any alarm bells, trigger any warning signals? Not for a second. In truth, it made me stand taller, pleased that I was capable, busy, and productive.

When I say my behavior wasn't normal the truth is, incredible as it may seem, is that it has always been normal for me (and for so many women I know). It didn't occur to me to explore a different way of being, a more effective way of operating, a kinder way of treating myself. I didn't know there was a different way. I truly did not know what I did not know.

I understand now that I could only choose something different when I became aware there is a choice. Being busy and productive held incredible significance for me. It meant I was okay, I was enough. As long as I kept achieving something, I *was* something! I pushed my body constantly, treating myself like a machine until my body couldn't sustain the constant expending without topping up my own resources. I thought I simply liked to be busy. Now I realize that my normal wasn't normal at all.

What is normal? Surely, normal is natural, balanced, and easy. I was none of these things in my relationship with myself and in my relationship with life. I completely missed the point that life needs balance; that we must balance activity with rest, work with leisure, doing with being. Even sleeping I had a busy mind moving through my never ending to do lists, punctuated with *should, must,* and *have to do.*

I was not aware. If you asked anybody about me it's likely they would have said. "She was wise beyond her years." (I heard this often since childhood—I was the responsible one in the family.) Before my diagnosis, I was compassionate, caring, clever, and capable—and I was incapable of being these things with myself. I could do them for those around me; my family, friends, patients, their significant others; all and sundry, but not myself.

The Second Slap

How could this be? The answer came a number of years following the first Big Slap. By this time, I had tried many interventions and though I was no longer bed-bound or housebound, my activity remained restricted. I managed to walk to the car, drive my kids to school, and repeat the same at the end of the school day but never managed anything beyond that. I was not getting any better. I was learning to manage, including the extreme pain which comes with fibromyalgia. Despite all my reading and researching, I still wasn't getting my life back.

I gave to all but I couldn't receive and I didn't realize that the root of the issue was with me. I did not know how to accept support. In truth, I didn't believe I deserved it. To me, asking for help was a sign of weakness, receiving support meant I wasn't coping, and was a judgement on my capabilities.

The second slap came when I realized that I didn't know it was okay for me to have needs. Awareness came, like a curtain being pulled back slowly, allowing light in. I felt dazed. I'd been in the dark, ignorant of my limiting beliefs for so long, it took time for me to get my head around it all.

Initially I felt shock. "That can't be true, don't be ridiculous,", my ego said. "Of course, you have needs and they get met!

The ego doesn't embrace change. The ego is the small, scared, wounded part of self, that does what it needs to survive and get on with things. It will always resist new concepts and anything that moves it beyond the limitations that it knows.

My ego said, "What a load of rubbish! That's just nonsense. You do just fine. You enjoy nice food, treat yourself to chocolate, you like your baths, you have a nice life and there's nothing you're left needing."

The slowly awakening, more conscious part of me ignored these platitudes and started to examine my behaviors, my thought patterns, and the *whys* behind my actions. This time was insightful, and it took me by surprise. It felt like an outsider; like a student in English class observing and analyzing the main characters' storyline.

The story started to fill out, to make sense, and I realized that I had gone through my first 35 years completely disconnected from me. I had become so adept at playing the role of what was expected of me I didn't realize I was living by somebody else's script. I moved through my life like an actor engrossed in playing the role.

I believed completely that this was my story and who I was. In this story, I had a self-designated role:

- I was the sensible one. Responsible and caring.
- I was the serious one, diligently determined to get everything right. I was the good girl at school, responsible helper at home, accessory caregiver to my siblings and my aging grandmother.
- And when it came time to choose a career nursing seemed a natural fit. It was the perfect role given my natural tendencies and caring, responsible nature. I love helping others. Being useful gave me a sense of purpose, of self, and of value.
- When I became a step mum, I readily took on the role of responsibility and continued when my own girls were born. I was the primary caregiver as my husband worked long hours and was often away.
- I was a loyal and trusting friend and sibling, always ready to help and offer assistance whenever it was needed.

The Gift of Illness

It took me a long time to appreciate my illness as a gift and to see the wisdom in my body's messages. It was a slow process. Like a toddler starting to walk I slowly built a relationship with myself. Getting to know who I was meant digging through the layers of expectations, responsibilities, and beliefs I'd taken on. Little by little, I peeled away the onion-like layers to discard the old programs and imprints that were never mine. My life often felt like an ill-fitting cloak as I figured out what was a good fit and what worked for the real me. A nearly debilitating illness is what it took for me to find my own clear, separate sense of self.

It's a journey that has overtime brought me back to health and brought me home to me. The real me. The me who knows she is deserving of all the love, support, and abundance the universe has to offer. The me who knows she is meant to receive in an equal and balanced way, relative to that which she gives out. I have finally learnt what it is to know unconditional love and accept myself; not because of what I do—simply because I AM.

I have discovered I'm not so serious anymore. I love more, have more joy in my life and happily hand over the reins to others without feeling I have to do it all myself and always be in control. It's refreshing, it's liberating.

I have learnt many things on my journey back to health and home to me. The most important I would like to share with you now, so you can begin to take the lead role in your own life, break through the glass ceilings keeping you stuck in a life that isn't working for you.

You are enough just as you are.

This is my message to women. Embrace your perfect imperfections and commit to being your own best friend. I share my story to help you conceive a new vision for you.

You see, I still love to help people. Now, my approach to health, both as a professional and a woman, includes a deeper appreciation and understanding of the complex nature of health; it is not only the absence of illness, it is about being healthy on a physical, mental, spiritual and emotional level. I now realize the important role our beliefs play in making us unwell and how a holistic approach to healing is what is really needed to return to wellness.

I realize now that wellness and wholeness, go hand in hand. It is about learning to come into a partnership with oneself, developing a relationship of ease, in order to correct any underlying, disease that may be present.

To correct any disease, there are many steps we must take but a core component, beyond nutrition, medicine, lifestyle changes, or any other positive action steps we may take to regain our health, is to learn to be at peace with our self. I believe this comes when we find our own place in the world and give permission to the real authentic self, perfect in all her imperfection, to shine through.

I want you to know you are more capable, wise, beautiful, and brilliant than you know. Give yourself permission to nurture your dreams, tune into the messages of your body and honor the yearnings of your soul. This is your one precious life. I invite you to come home to yourself. Uncover your real story and allow yourself to conceive a vision for your life that is rich and abundant and all that you deserve. When each of us commit to this in our own hearts and our own lives, we pave the way for our sisters, friends, our daughters to own their own unique beauty, honor their brilliance, and live their truth.

I'll close by sharing a few words of wisdom written after a discussion between my sister and I (after some vino!). We had asked, "What advice would you give your younger self?" Oh, how the tongue loosens, and the wisdom flows when aided by a glass of wine or two!!

- Believe in yourself.
- Always be true to you.
- Never ever, ever give up.
- Fight for what you believe in.
- Honor your truth, nobody really knows it but you.
- Live the dream.
- It's your life, only you can make it happen.

- Stop telling yourself you can't, because you bloody well can.
- The only one stopping you is *you*.
- Always listen to your gut, it knows the truth.
- Never ever ignore that truth is your most powerful ally.
- Talk about the stuff that matters, stuff no one talks about.
- Learn something new every day.
- Have an open mind on everything.
- Never judge another. *There but for the grace of God go I.*
- If you believe in it, fight for it.
- If it feels right, it is right.
- Stop resisting. It is what it is. Accept it!
- When you're with someone, really be present. Be there.
- Your friendships and relationships should make you smile, think, or want to be a better person.
- Always be thankful for the blessings that you have.
- If it makes you happy go for it!
- A life lived in fear is a life wasted. What will you choose? Fear or love? Live it, love it, the time is now.
- Keep it consistent. Go confidently toward your dreams

There are countless different paths you can take to nurture the spirit and help you find a purpose. There is no right or wrong. Listen to your heart. Live in harmony with your head, heart, and spirit. As you do your health improves, your happiness grows, and your contentment with life and self abound.

AUTHOR CLAIRE RYAN HEATLEY

HEALTH RECOVERY COACH, WOMEN'S EMPOWERMENT COACH, SPEAKER

Claire is a wife, mum, and step mum who believes that the best gift we can give ourselves and teach our children is how to honor self-care and nurturing. She firmly believes that it is the quality of the relationships we have with ourselves and with those with whom we journey through life is what really matters.

Claire is an inspiring, natural born leader and has worked in the field of health and wellness for over 20 years.

Her passion is supporting women through the challenges of chronic illness and chronic stress, so they can reclaim their health, step into their power, and live their precious life as it's meant to be lived.

She specializes in ME/ CFS and Fibromyalgia, supporting women to return to an enlivened sense of wholeness and vitality as she did from these and other chronic debilitating conditions, using her unique *Health Accelerator Recovery Programme*. She is here to be of service and knows no greater joy then to support others on their recovery journey.

Claire is a co-host on the *Loveheart And Soul Community Radio Show*, broadcasting two shows, *Honouring your Body and its Divine Body Wisdom* and *The Golden Keys to Empowerment*, where she shares her knowledge and wisdom, and offers support to live call in audiences.

Connect with the Author. . .

Website
www.claireryanheatley.com
www.overcomingmeandcfs.com

Social Media
Facebook: https://m.facebook.com/claireryanheatley
Facebook: https://www.facebook.com/groups/459131781118208
Instagram: https://www.instagram.com/overcomingmeandcfs/
Twitter: https://mobile.twitter.com/overcomingmecfs

Blog Talk Radio:
http://www.blogtalkradio.com/caroline-sakuracrystallineloveheart

Email
Claire@overcomingmeandcfs.com
claire@claireryanheatley.com

"Leadership is a mother who will break through every barrier in life, no matter what the circumstance, to get out of the darkness and into the light for the sake of herself and her children." ~ Jacqueline D. Pickering

Blessings in Disguise

JACQUELINE D. PICKERING

I was recently in a car accident that became a wake-up call for me. As you read my story, you may see yourself through my life. For all mothers and their children out there who have many obstacles to face in life, causing you to feel trapped, worthless and have lost hope, this story is dedicated to you. I feel so grateful that I am here today writing this story for you. Remember, you can pick yourself back up as long you are breathing and alive. I don't think I could have done it without my family

Raised by parents from a third world country, I lived an isolated life. Having friends or going out was not an option. The one thing I clearly remember is that I was never allowed to ask for anything; my opinion did not matter. I grew up believing that women are to get married and have children. When I finally met the love of my life, I felt a sense of freedom within me that was hard to control. I feared it was too good to be true, a fear that proved to be prophetic.

My twenty-year marriage was not what I expected to be. It was full of physical, emotional and financial abuse that was a serious challenge for the kids and I to escape from. I prayed to God to show me a way out of this trapped environment.

One Saturday morning we found the strength to make it end. The kids and I had arrived home from grocery shopping. I put the groceries on the kitchen floor and, telling the kids that we would put the groceries away later, I lay down for a short nap.

I was awakened by my 14-year-old son's screams. He was in my daughter's room yelling, "Mom! Mom! Hurry!"

I ran as fast as I could and arrived in time to hear my husband say to my 13-year-old daughter, "If you ever raise your voice to me again, I will kill you."

He then left the house, and I rushed to my daughter.

Her face was tinged blue as she kneeled on her knees, clinging to my son's legs, crying desperately for help. She begged for us to leave and never come back. As I comforted and calmed her, she struggled to tell me her father had strangled her with one hand while punching her with the other. I couldn't breathe or speak from the shock. I was shaking so drastically that I fell on my knees. All I could say out loud was, "I promise never again."

We took a change of clothes and headed to my mother's house. I knew we had a long, hard journey ahead of us to recover and get back on our feet. I had no choice but to call the police and have him charged and arrested for what he did. This was uncalled for, unacceptable, and forever unforgiven.

Life as a Single parent:

Moving in to my mother's home was our only option as the kids and I had lost everything; our clothes, furniture, our savings, and even the car. It felt like life was over. I was scared, hurt, and felt lost. I wanted to be dead rather than alive. I felt that death would take all my problems away. After all, how could I, who could not even take care of herself, take care of teenagers who have been abused by their father? It was hard trying to stand on my own two feet. Then I would look into my children's eyes, I would watch them when they were sleeping, and I was reminded that they are my reason for being here. I remember that first night at my Mother's home that I crept into their bedroom and kissed them both on their forehead.

I whispered in their ears as they slept, "Don't worry. You're safe now." The nights that followed were long, and I found sleep with difficulty. I often heard my daughter and son calling out my name for help. I would rush to their room and they would be sound asleep. Every night, while they slept, I would kiss them on their forehead and whisper, "It's ok. I'll take care of you."

I took on a second job working 80 hours a week to provide for myself and the children. I prayed twice a day asking the Lord to heal my children from the pain and suffering they had experienced and to save them from further trauma. When within the year I lost my full-time job, and was left with minimal income, I had no choice but to beg family for their support. Without my family, I would not be here today.

I searched through websites, newspapers, and postings. Finally, I found a job with an investigation company as a translator. The relief that I felt at that moment is indescribable. Six months into the job, I was once again laid off. They no longer needed my services in translating documents. I had not been employed long enough to recover financially and became desperate. I literally spent eight hours a day every day looking for another job. And my efforts paid off when I did find work with a reputable company where I would assist patients to manage their diabetes. Soon after I started, I knew that this was my forever job and quit my second job. I couldn't handle 80 hours a week.

The Summer Night when Life Changed Again

It was the night of June 29, 2015 at approximately 5:00 in the evening. The sun still shone brightly. The temperature was warm as can be and a nice breeze flowed ever so gently. As the weather was beautiful, the children, and I decided to go for a nice drive. My daughter was the driver, my son the passenger up front and I was in the backseat. We drove up to Burnaby Mountain where we knew there was a stunning and breathtaking view overlooking the lower mainland. We enjoyed a peaceful time admiring the view, then decided to head home.

We switched drivers for the ride back and it was my son was driving us home. By popular vote we decided to complete our lovely journey by stopping for ice cream.

My son pulled out to make a left turn at the signal light. We were hit head on by a young driver in a Trail Sun blazer traveling over 130 km an hour as he ran the red light.

I don't remember the collision. My first memory after deciding on ice cream is regaining consciousness lying on the ground with a paramedic yelling at me not to move.

The sirens were so loud, there were people all around us shouting. Then I picked out my son's voice from the crowd. I saw him pacing back and forth as close to me as they would let him come.

He screamed, "Mom! Mom you're alive!! Monique and I thought you were dead! Oh my God, Mom! Thank God you're alive!" He then kneeled, and came close enough to hold my hand.

"We got hit Mom. There's a couple that landed under our car but don't worry Mom. We will be ok now that you are alive."

I once again felt my purpose in life, my children needed me to be here as it was evident that I was their safety blanket. The feeling was so heartfelt that I burst into tears until I could no longer cry tears.

We finally made it to the hospital where CT scans were done on each one of us over a period of 15 hours. Those were long and painful hours. Thankfully, we had no broken bones, only bruises. My daughter experienced neck and back pain; my son's stomach swelled up five inches outward. I couldn't move my neck, shoulders, and knees due to the swelling. I prayed asking God to help us through this.

At first it felt like as if it was a nightmare but hour after hour it was apparent that it was reality. Laying on my stretcher bed, I heard my son crying to his grandmother, feeling guilty as he was the driver.

Then a nurse came in to say that my daughter was scared and asking for her brother. My poor son, in shock and hurt, went back and forth between his sister and I to comfort us and make sure we were ok.

We were blessed, and yet, I prefer not to remember the next few weeks. My mind was spinning, and I kept running the same thoughts over and over again through my mind, "Why us? Why did we need to suffer this much in life? what have we done to deserve this? Have we not suffered enough? Now what do I do? I need a car to get to work, but I can't move my neck so I can't drive. I have no money to buy a car. I need the income, but how can I work? Without money, I can't feed the kids, I have to work."

I felt like a darkness had closed in on me. I could no longer see a light at the end of the tunnel in life.

My mother, God bless her heart, bought me a used car and charged in to her credit card. My poor mother is on a fixed income and she couldn't afford that charge on her credit card, which made me feel even worse. Thankfully, my sister who lives overseas, sent her some money to help. My brothers as well, donated money to help us. I can't say this often enough, without my family, I would not be here today.

Two weeks of not working and not getting paid made me feel desperate for money. I went back to work. I didn't care about my health or wellbeing, all I wanted was to provide for my children. It was my only logical solution.

I woke every morning and took my medications for my neck so I could drive to work. Having a concussion did not help my situation. One of the main symptoms of having a bad concussion is an inability to handle noise. Between being on the phone and having to interact with people all day, work was challenging. I put a pillow and blanket in my car so that during my coffee and lunch breaks I could nap in the car. I parked in the underground parkade where it was quiet and peaceful. These naps made it possible for me to get through the day.

I had no appetite, my neck was killing me, and my head throbbed constantly. Would I rather have stayed home and let my body heal?

Was it the right decision? Month after month of working while suffering a temporary concussion led to it becoming a sustained concussion. Going back to work made things worse for me. Slowly I became less productive at work and more ill, so much that staff members noticed. My productivity went from 98 percent to 40 percent.

A year after going back to work I lost my job once again leaving me in a financial bind. Interestingly enough, my last day of work was on my birthday. I drove home crying. I couldn't stop crying. I was scared, panicked, and feeling hopeless. I had never felt so hopeless, so much more than I can even put into words.

I'm not sure how, but I made it home. I sat down with my mother and told her, "I can't take it anymore. I have no purpose in life. I'm tired of suffering. I don't have any more strength within me to carry on. I just want to go to heaven."

The next thing I knew I was taken to the emergency by my mother and brother. There I was given sedatives to calm me and was referred to a psychiatrist for a follow up. My appointment with the psychiatrist was a must as it was my only hope for recovery. I was diagnosed with Post Traumatic Stress Disorder. The combination of spousal abuse, the struggles to pick up our lives, the car accident, and then the year spent pushing myself instead of allowing my body to recover had led to PTSD and a severe case of depression. My diagnosis included an anxiety and panic disorder.

The psychiatrist sent me to a psychologist for follow-up treatment and a more thorough assessment.

The assessment showed my memory to be severely impacted, my perception to be slow, my ability to process information low, and that I have the capability of a grade 4 student. Of course, none of this was what I wanted to hear.

The testing confirmed that I was unable to work. I returned to my doctor with a letter from the psychiatrist and psychologist to show that I need to be under disability.

Disability became my status at last.

My current life:

Today I realize that all along I've had blessings in disguise. My daughter being strangled was a way out of the abusive and trapped environment the kids and I could never leave. My losing jobs over and over again was because of my inability to work due to PTSD. The car accident was exactly that, an accident. And yes, it became the grand finale where I was forced to stop working.

God knew I could no longer work. I'm not sure why this was the only way I could be stopped from working, but I accept it now. All was God showing me the way to healing and resting in life. Sometimes we suffer so much in life that the reasoning behind everything is not apparent. But the day comes where it is realized that it is all part of a journey getting to the light at the end of the tunnel.

Leadership through Recovery

There is a light at the end of this story, and the book you are reading is proof. After the wreck, I was tossed and tattered, but realizing that I had gone through this experience for a reason. That reason is to help other women who have had their children exposed to violence by their father figure, be stronger in their walk and prayer.

The recovery has been hard, no doubt about it, but I now realize that I was chosen for this experience. I can feel the power within myself today. Are you wondering what this has to do with leadership? To me, I've been lead to this place in my life and sharing my story is how I am able to lead others who need to know that there is a light at the end of the tunnel. It comes with keeping faith, even when the why is not apparent.

AUTHOR JACQUELINE D. PICKERING

I am a single mother of two beautiful young adult children who are my life, pride and joy. A mother who, without any doubt, will do all that needs to be done to survive in life. I believe that there are no problems in life but rather situations, and each situation has a solution.

This story is dedicated to all mothers and children who are and have gone through so much trauma in life. My hope is that my story will inspire women and children to not give up hope but rather walk through the burning stones in life as you will survive.

Connect with the Author. . .

Social Media
Facebook: http://facebook.com/jacqueline.pickering3
Twitter: https://twitter.com/humanbehaviours
LinkedIn: https://www.linkedin.com/in/jacqueline-pickering-58875865/
Instagram: https://www.instagram.com/wishingwell2013/
Email: Jacqueline.pickering2@gmail.com

"Your past does not define you, it simply informs and gives you the courage, the strength, and resilience to move forward and succeed beyond your wildest dreams!" ~ *Susan Robichaud*

A Life's Lesson in Courage and Resilience

SUSAN ROBICHAUD

*E*very life has a series of defining moments that can re-shape our experience and change our direction. These moments have a huge impact on our choices and on both personal and professional development. These moments aren't always recognizable when they are happening and it can sometimes feel like the world is ending or that we just can't go on when we are going through them. Some of these moments can be positive while others might be negative. Nonetheless, everyone has them and we all deal in our own unique way.

For me, the defining moment that shaped and changed the direction of my now 16-year-old business was when my son took sick. He joined our family when he was 18 months old, and we soon discovered that something wasn't right with him. After taking him to see a few specialists, he was diagnosed with FASD (Fetal Alcohol Spectrum Disorder) at age three and now lives with permanent brain damage and has since developed epilepsy to boot. FASD can happen when a pregnant woman drinks any type of alcohol. The amount of drinking that occurs at specific periods of the pregnancy is what determines the levels of learning disabilities, sensory issues, and behavioral, mood, and physical challenges.

This has been quite a journey for our family. My personal motto is, "If one child lives with any type of syndrome or challenge, be it FASD, Autism, Anxiety or any, the whole family lives with it, too.". As I write this, I could not be more grateful for the support and assistance we have had to make his life and ours a little easier.

It is true we experience many challenges and are never sure what any specific day will bring. There are equally as many special moments. We simply could not see our life without this awesome kid!

For years, I worked behind the scenes with my clients, focusing on developing, maintaining and managing their website and marketing. I absolutely loved my work and things were good. I was very busy and loved every minute of it, however, last year, when my son got really sick and started having epileptic seizures on a daily basis, I found myself having to put my business on the back burner to care for him. This was really tough, I wanted and tried to be everything to everyone, and that's when the defining moment happened.

I remember the day, just as if it were yesterday. Sitting in my office, tears running down my face, transitioning my final client on to another provider who could serve them in the way that they needed, it hit me like a ton of bricks. It was time to re-design my business model, to re-focus my energy, and turn this situation around. This was the moment when I made a conscious decision to design my business in such a way that it would suit my lifestyle and family situation. To put all the pieces in order with a personal support system who could help with my son and to finally create structure, systems, and strategies to support the continued growth of my business.

Quitting was no option. I knew, with the experience and skills I gathered during the last 16 years, I had all I needed to continue doing what I loved. I wanted only to tweak it a bit. I also knew, with every fiber of my being, that I could make it happen—and so I did!

Today I feel more aligned with my business and my purpose. I have a renewed passion for my work, and because of this experience, I am well positioned and qualified to work with groups of small business owners helping them to reach their desired goals and achieve more success with their own business and marketing than they ever dreamed to be possible.

Thankfully, my son is doing much better these days, and I have a support system in place so that I can focus on my new business model during the day and be there for my family evenings and weekends. Granted I am still available when and if things get tough for him again, however, with my business now being primarily online, I have the liberty of working from wherever I need to.

My new favorite quote is: "If it is important to you, you will find a way, if it is not, you will find excuses." The defining moments are the driving force behind the reshaping of our experiences and the changing of the direction for the better.

My motivation and inspiration comes from my son, who continues to thrive through life no matter what challenges may be placed before him. I share this story with you because from where I sit today, looking back on the many defining moments of my now 47 years of existence, I see that whatever you want to accomplish in your life, be it professional or personal, all it really takes is a plan coupled with focused, determined action and consistent communication.

If I can do it, you can do it too!

AUTHOR SUSAN ROBICHAUD

DIRECT RESPONSE MARKETING MENTOR

Susan Robichaud is the founder of the Marketing Engine for your business, the most comprehensive mentorship package/process and system available today! This training, coaching and development process helps small business owners build a solid foundation that includes structure, systems, and strategies. Her primary goal as a Direct Response Marketing Expert and Mentor, is to encourage her clients to take focused actions daily so they earn their worth, share their value, and spread their message through to as many people as humanly and digitally possible. She plays full out and teach her clients all that she has learned and continues to learn in the evolving world of marketing.

As a mom and in business, Susan leads by example, teaching and motivating small business owners to reach their goals and achieve more success than they ever thought was possible.

Connect with the Author. . .

Website: Axion Marketing, Inc. www.MarketingEngine.ca
30-day Challenge: http://marketingengine.ca/en/gainmomentum

"It's simply not enough to attempt leadership without accepting all humans as good and building them up from there." ~ Carla Wynn Hall

The Acceptance Principle of Leadership

A Unique Approach to Activating the Best in People

CARLA WYNN HALL (COMPILER)

I remember my first real job as if it were yesterday. During my Senior year of high-school I would leave at 11:00 and go to McDonald's working in a Co-Op program. My amazing job flipping burgers taught me the most valuable lesson of my life.

The Accept Principle of Leadership is a unique approach to activate the best in people. But, I was not treated with acceptance, nor was the best brought out in me by the boss. I learned the opposite, in fact.

Today I am a best-selling author and women's writing coach. I fully enjoy using this technique on the women I work with. Showing women their best, even when they can't see it, is the essence of the leadership dynamic of acceptance and allowance. With these words, I am a better coach. Let's rewind.

Many men and women start their work career at a fast food restaurant. Some hate it, others love it. Some stay in the restaurant business their entire life while others moved on, perhaps to join the military. One's first experience working a job forms the foundation, providing lessons in ethics, respect, and human potential. My time in fast food was the greatest gift of my life. The lessons are impeccable.

Acceptance Leadership for Activating the Best in People

I experienced several food service jobs, in different restaurants, and every one of them resulted in my promotion into management. I never had a big ambition to be a manager, nor did I consider myself to be a leader. I did know this: I wanted everyone to be their best. Because I saw my team members through a lens of total acceptance, I was able to progress easily into higher positions.

On the personal side, in 1996, I remarried the father of my two youngest sons. After a bad ending to an even worse marriage in 1990, I chose to give that marriage another try. In 1997 my middle son was born and my life changed again. I knew that I wanted to be a mother who was present in her children's lives. My oldest son was 10 when Joshua was born, so there is a bit if distance between them in age.

As I explored working from home options, I chose as a stop-gap to once again work for a fast food restaurant, a popular regional chain called Jack's.

"Carla, would you like to be the store manager of the new restaurant?" The General Manager of Jack's surprised me with this question one morning.

Beaming with excitement, I told him I would love to do this.

I had no clue, I mean *zero clue*, how to go about training men and women from different walks of life, in how to start out a new job. I knew my skills were top-notch. I knew I was good at all the team positions. I also knew that my greatest strength is that I only see the good in people.

He doubled my pay, and I completely trained an entire crew for his new store. My inner-leader came forth as I saw the diamond of worth hidden inside of me. It was at this job where I learned how to take a group of people, all from unique backgrounds, and lead them into deep, profound success.

Acceptance Leadership to Bring out the Best

As I trained the crew members (on every area from being a cashier, to making homemade buttermilk biscuits), I learned from them and from the experience to deepen my leadership philosophy. Everyone has the same opportunity to rise to management. Opening a new Jack's restaurant taught me that people who take jobs cooking at a fast food chain have different (often limited) hopes, dreams, and ambitions. I learned that having a celebration with every success helps them to feel celebrated at the next crossroad.

and one of the training techniques I implemented at Jack's was the Switch Technique. I purchased a whistle from the sporting goods store and used it to cause the team members to switch their position. Each one of the crew knew what their next position would be when they heard the whistle. The back-line cooks would wash their hands and go to the front to run a register. The biscuit maker would clean up and go to the drive through window, and so on. This technique trained every team member on the other's jobs and earned my crew an award just weeks after the store opened. I was elated and validated.

Every Human Being Deserves the Same Chance to Win

Today I work with women who want to write books. Some of the women I have had the opportunity to help have serious disabilities such as Cerebral Palsy and Spina Bifida. I use the same principles with them today as I did with the crew at Jack's. Every human being deserves to be treated as if they are their best. Every human being has the same chance at victory as the next human being. This is leadership through acceptance.

My contribution to this book is a three-part mini-lesson I call Idea Alchemy. It will help you excel at your current job or career. The Idea

Alchemy lessons also will show you how to take any situation and become a leader. You may feel that life has dealt you a bad hand as it relates to money or income, but there are lessons in every situation. Restaurant management taught me that when you believe in another and see their greatness before they see it, you have planted positive seeds in their hearts.

Idea Alchemy for Leadership Development

This lesson asks you to start a journal to build your leadership skills in any career you choose.

Within the journal write these three questions:
1. What type of career am I working in today?
2. How many people work around me?
3. What are my day-to-day activities?

Next, identify any thoughts you have about improvement and build these thoughts out further. Use these questions to start your thinking:
1. What is the first area you would improve?
2. What are three steps you can take to make this happen?
3. How will your idea improve the company and yourself?

To truly be a leader who uses Acceptance Leadership as a core value, you must be prepared to always voice your opinions on improvement. When you input positive visions into your company and into your own life, things start to get better and you have a skill that lasts a lifetime.

The Cupcake Party

At the end of our training time together, my crew was amazing. They had not only developed the skills needed to work every area of the business, but they formed their own support system. I gave them worksheets and homework during the training, and we always celebrated. I learned about their reasons for working at a fast food restaurant and heard about their dreams and ambitions.

Soon enough, the end and the beginning arrived.

We opened at 5:30 am and the opening crew had to be there at 4:00 am to start the biscuits, get the ovens hot, and begin cooking. I brought several boxes of cake mix, and cans of frosting. In addition to cooking biscuits, we made cupcakes for the crew and for the customers. When the rest of the breakfast crew arrived, we had our first celebration. I presented each of them with a blue-ribbon and a cupcake, telling them that I considered them to be part of my family and how proud I was of their individual accomplishments. This included me telling them very specific qualities I appreciated and noticed about them.

When the lunch crew came in we did the same thing. We celebrated their victories together. The same with the night shift, and again with the other managers. I expressed my deep gratitude to the store supervisor for the opportunity and was offered a higher position, which I refused. I refused it because I wanted more—to be able to raise the son I was carrying in my womb.

Leadership is in Your DNA

No matter your situation, or the hand life has dealt to you, practicing acceptance in all you do is the key to truly being a leader. We all walk side-by-side in a human experience like no other. Look at every person you meet and see the best in them. The more you see the best in others, the more that others will see the best in you.

AUTHOR CARLA WYNN HALL

Carla Wynn Hall has compiled number one International best-selling books since 2014 with the publishing of *Empowered Women of Social Media: Finding Global Unity in Social Communities*. In this book series, she asked women to submit a chapter about how they found unity with people from different cultures and countries through using Facebook or another social network.

She built a group in 2010 that grew to over 25,000 members within three years. Simultaneously with the publishing of her first book, *Rock Bottom Chronicles: The Paradigm Shift that Saved my Life*, she began to see the healing power of writing out a painful story, and had the idea of opening a multi-author book for women; specifically, to the members of her Facebook group.

Empowered Women of Social Media has two volumes and they are available on Amazon.com along with Carla Wynn Hall's other published works. The first compilation was such a giant success that she placed 100 authors, 20 endorsers, and five corporate sponsors in the book. Within 24 hours the book soared to number one in Canada, Australia, and the USA. She intentionally placed the book in the Self-Help Motivation category on Amazon, one of the top Amazon categories with books such as *The Secret* and *Lean In* being at the top. Her reasoning was to challenge the women to achieve empowerment that came from being part of a best-selling book that competed with books published by established, global leaders.

Carla Wynn Hall has a deep passion of helping women heal their memories. Her writings focus on past pain transmutation and writing out a new story to heal the old one. Through allowing women to have permission to say their story out loud, she truly believes the memory changes, and therefore the pain associated with the memory is healed.

How to Bend the Universe: Magic Lessons for Living an Imperfect Experience is her latest release and will be available on Christmas day, 2017 in Kindle and paperback. In her fourth contribution to literacy, Carla Wynn Hall has created a way for women to finally break-out of modality madness and see the truth of attraction. Magic is a word which has held taboo association. In her book, she flips this notion on its head by showing readers that simple magic tricks can ease the burden of perfection. Society is shifting into acceptance after years of division and harsh requirements upon each other as a human race. *How to Bend the Universe* brings the element of play into the picture as it creates a new definition of life.

Carla Wynn Hall is the mother of three sons, Logan, Joshua, and Nickolas, and a grandmother of three grandchildren Lilly, Chloe, and Alex. Together she and her husband, Bear Hall have six grandchildren. Her deepest desire is to become a New York Times best-selling author and retire with royalty income while building a trust fund for her children and grandchildren.

Carla is the creator of the *Launch and Learn* system for women who want to build a business and make money, through self-publishing their books. She is also the founder of the *Lucrative Self-Publishing Night School* where she teaches women how to take steps toward being an author, in the hours of their availability.

Connect with the Author. . .

Website: http://www.carlawynnhall.com
Social Media
  Facebook: http://www.facebook.com/carlawynnhall
  Twitter: @carlawynnhall
  LinkedIn: http://www.linkedin.com/in/carlawynnhall
Email: carla@carlawynnhall.com

"We need to move beyond the idea that girls can be leaders and create the expectation that they should be leaders." ~ Condeleezza Rice

Leadership begins at the Kitchen Table

CYNTHIA BEYER

I vividly remember my first exposure to leadership. It was an ordinary evening around the kitchen table. My parents discussed who would take my brothers over to the 4-H meeting that night. My brothers had joined our local 4-H Club, the Nordick Nymphs. Our group meet at the Nordick Township Hall in rural Minnesota. The creaky old wooden building lacked indoor plumbing. Excitement gleamed in my small, 8-year-old eyes as this would be my first official meeting, and tonight I would become a member of the Nordick Nymphs 4-H Club. Even though, the couches groaned and moaned and *eeked* with our weight (to this day, I believe mice lived in the couches), my excitement could not be contained.

In the past, I had attended meetings, patiently sitting on my Mom's lap, listening intently to the flow of the meeting. Awestruck by how smoothly it ran, the meeting flowed like a river, consistent as the leaders used Robert's Rules of Parliamentary Procedure. The Call to order, the motions made and seconded, the voting, the action items, the demonstrations and project talks, the adjournment, all had a rhythm calling me to action.

Those early 4-H meetings gave me a taste of how a leader runs a meeting. I vowed, as I sat there in a dress made by my great aunts from their leftover fabric, that I would be President and run my meeting just as efficiently as the older girls did.

By the time I was 11, I was the President and leading the group. Working my way through all the offices gave me confidence to participate and lead our small group.

4-H also taught life skills. Participating as the narrator at talent show completion and competing in the Radio Public Speaking contests gave me confidence to speak in public. Sewing and baking and exhibiting these accomplishments at our County Fair gave me valuable life skills. Showing my pigs, chickens and beef steers gave me strength of character, especially when the beef steers ran away with me hanging on for dear life. My parents made a choice to have their children join 4-H. All these leadership traits and qualities began at our kitchen table.

Children's Exposure to leadership should begin as early as possible.

As parents, we are the primary caregivers for our children. We teach them to talk, walk, and eat and provide all the basic human skills for their ages. As they advance and are ready for more, we give it. They learn that we, their parents, are the pack leader and that it's our job show them how to lead.

Talk about your Lessons Learned at work with your children

During my career, I worked at an engineering company. One of our best practices consisted of doing a *Lessons Learned* review upon completion of a project or proposal. Lessons Learned provided a powerful process to reflect on what worked well and what did not work well for a project or a specific proposal.

In the throes of deadlines, we rarely take the time to verify that the methodologies used are the most effective tools for the project. When we take a step back and review Lessons Learned, we can see areas to improve. A leader will take the time to reflect on what worked well and what did not with a project. A leader will review this process with team to examine how to obtain the best results for next time.

Using Lessons Learned as a leader can be invaluable for when a project goes awry. For instance, I was part of a team that recently pitched several proposals to provide full city operations to various clients. We prepared our standard proposal, rehashed the same language that had worked in the past, and submitted it. In hindsight, two glaring missteps occurred, we failed to fully evaluate the client's actual needs and the client's budget. We did not listen to the needs of the customer. Without reflecting and examining why we lost the contract, we would not have discovered what should be corrected next time around.

After we lost the proposal, when my sons asked me their usual question, "How was your day Mom?" A scowl slowly spread across my face as I related the story about the award of the contract going to another vendor. The boys had seen me put in late nights and early morning hours to assemble the information to complete our proposal. The boys had seen me take emergency phone calls as the team assembled the missing bits of information. To have lost the bid, created frustration and anger in me. But when we talked about the project and what had gone wrong and what we could have done better, it opened up a new venue of conversation. This allowed my sons to learn the value of Lessons Learned in school projects and in life and working well with others.

Leadership needs to take the time to do a 20/20 hindsight review. When I went through our Lessons Learned with my sons, I gave them a tool they could use to see why they received the grades that they had received or not received in class. Lessons Learned provided a path for creating different outcomes in their own projects.

Get your children involved at an early age in group activities.

As a leader, you head up a group of people. I strongly believe unless a person has learned to play team sports or participated in group activities, they may fail to learn how to work in a team environment. Being part of a team teaches about different personalities. They learn how to play well with others. They learn how to win and be successful. And they learn to lose and be successful.

As soon as the boys were old enough to participate in Cub Scouts, we had them join. Being a part of a team teaches children to interact with others. In Cub Scouts, they learned to work together for a common cause. For instance, in the fall when they had the food drive, they worked as a team to collect, sort, and deliver the food donations for those in need. They realized one person could not do it all but with the efforts of the joint collective, they accomplished the task in no time. In Cub Scouts, the adults serve in the leadership roles, teaching the boys how to come together for the common efforts. But in Boy Scouts, boys lead the meetings and determine the activities. Providing a cosmos for children to experiment in leadership, provides an opportunity to learn different styles.

Sports offer another leadership opportunity. My sons played lacrosse in their younger years. My youngest son was the goalie. I told him he was the leader on the field because he had the advantage of seeing the entire field from his viewpoint. Thus, it was his responsibility to see and direct the players into position. Over time, those early lessons gave him the confidence to see how to adjust and realign his own teams, whether for joint physics projects or marching band.

Begin your leadership lessons early with your children. Talk about your leadership lessons with your children. Get your children involved at an early age in group activities. Our jobs as parents allows us the once in a lifetime opportunity to craft an individual who can impact the world in a positive way. Imagine the difference we can create in the new leaders for the world if we embark on this leadership journey with our children.

AUTHOR CYNTHIA BEYER

Ms. Beyer is a recovering attorney. She grew up on a farm in northwestern Minnesota, the second oldest of eight children. After graduating from high school, Ms. Beyer attended high school for a year in the Philippines. Upon her return, she attended the University of North Dakota for her undergraduate education and the University of North Dakota School of Law. She has practiced as an attorney for the past twenty-eight years.

Ms. Beyer is a John Maxwell Certified Speaker, Coach and Trainer. Ms. Beyer holds an Advanced Communicator Silver from Toastmasters International. In her free time, she skis, hikes, road bikes, and enjoys the Colorado lifestyle.

Earlier this year, Ms. Beyer first book, *Blow Your Nose, Pull Up Your Socks, and Get on With It! Five Keys to Success Single Parenting*, was published and serves as a keystone for her programs in support of professionals who are single parents.

Connect with the Author. . .

Social Media:
Linkedin: https://www.linkedin.com/in/cynthia-beyer-b3b0a95/

"Through forgiveness, love and validation I was able to grow from a very wounded child to an empowered woman." ~ *Liz*

Leadership Through Love

ELIZABETH HASSAN

*T*oday I feel that my role as a leader was well-hidden; behind the pain and constant need to give to others, I grew my leadership wings. Through relentless love and belief of others, I finally have realized the power within me, to lead through love. This is my story.

My father, a brick layer and my mother, a well-respected legal secretary and Paralegal, worked hard for their living. I and my siblings were all given the privilege of going to private schooling, primary and secondary. I now know this probably placed a strong burden on the family. Sadly, my father became an alcoholic and at what time of his life I do not know, all I remember as a young child is an aggressive drunk, antagonistic towards my mother. One argument that stands strong in my memory is of my mother asking my father to please eat his dinner. He became angry and said, "You know what I think of this dinner!" and threw his plate through the kitchen window. I distinctly remember standing absolutely still, frozen with intense fear, uncertain about what was going to happen next.

My only constant memory is of arguing and yelling. I would stand beside my mother as if I was programmed to go into protective mode to ensure that he would not hurt her. I have another strong memory of my childhood that is sitting up most nights beside my mother on the couch. No TV. No sound. Waiting and waiting, dreading to hear the sound of my father's car. A horrible fear would pour over me. The anticipation, the not knowing was the worst: was he going to walk in the door and start screaming and yelling at my mother or siblings?

Today I have finally found some independence from the memories and have used my new found emotional freedom to visit the UK (alone) to meet the family of Sarah, who was a young woman I cared for through her terminal illness. I honestly didn't know how I would survive watching her die, but my friends kept reminding me that I am an Angel. Leadership is part of the journey of love.

My Childhood was Void of Love

I have no memory of any parent saying, "I Love You," or for that matter as a little girl even seeing it. I grew up blaming my mother for not leaving my father and could not understand as a child why she would allow this to happen to her and my siblings.

Why was I the protector of the family? How did I manage it? Where did the strength come from? All I had come to know was that I was Mum to my siblings and my mother. I was the protector of our family. I was not given the chance to be a child, I was tormented.

I was unable to bring friends home. Why would I? How could I explain my father's drinking and rage? To me, all my other school friends lived in a different world. I could only somehow fake living in their world. At a young age, I learned to hide the sadness I felt and the abuse that was within our four walls and kept on moving through school life as if all was fine. I was envious of these other families.

"Mum, why won't you leave him?" I asked.

My mother looked down at me, thus this small, scattered childhood memory goes. I gather I was very young, and she said, "I will never leave your father."

My heart and soul were now gone from my body. I had only myself. I do not have any recollection of my sister who is only six years my junior, being anywhere within the walls of our home or out at school or around the house playing. Where was she? I know now she was there but how cruel is the brain to block that one precious memory and to never know any fun or growing experiences with her?

I have a few scattered memories of my brother. I remember times of yelling and seeing the look of terror on his face and I would stand beside him or in front of him so that the barrage of abuse would stop or that he would not get hit. I don't know, nor can I tell you from any memory, how I got away without being hurt by my Father.

Did I have some protective barrier around me or was I a strong-willed child? Was I just now solely the mother of the household and had to stand tall? Standing tall was scary. I was a fearful child.

I could not have been more than nine or ten as these memories I write are of the primary school years of my life. I never knew from one day to the next if someone would be hurt or if it would be a night of complete screaming and insults to us all. Why was my father's anger so deep and intense towards his family?

What did I do wrong Daddy?

Adult Liz has seen a psychologist for two years to unravel my brain and sort out why I cannot remember the so called normal memories children have. I don't remember my bedroom or anything about the room, the bed, any ornaments. Nothing. I don't remember where my siblings slept. I don't remember seeing my siblings coming and going from home, but I do remember I was in charge and had to prepare meals at night because my parents were working.

I don't remember walking to school. I don't remember a lot of classmates in school photos, worse I don't remember even having the pictures taken year by year. I don't remember Christmas of any year or birthdays until my 16th. I don't remember what I ate at school for lunch. I don't remember any of my teachers. I don't remember the inside of any of my classrooms. I don't remember any of the other homes we lived in, only the one., My siblings can remember the others and they are younger than me.

I don't remember my Grandmother. I look, I study her face in an old picture. She is foreign to me, yet the only memory I have of her is a figure walking down the pathway to a house I don't remember anything inside of. She stops walking, puts her hands behind her back to hide the fact that always have lollies (lollipop) for me. Why can I not see you or your love, Nana in your face in the picture I have of you? How could that memory be erased?

Was my life as a child so unknowingly abusive that the adult Liz has lost all memory? I know through sessions with a psychologist that my memories are there, but they are embedded deeply, so much so that even he as a professional said, "There is no reason for you to remember." In one session with him I closed my eyes and with the psychologist guiding my thoughts, we took little Lizzie home. I tucked her into bed, I told her she was safe and no one could hurt her because I was here and I would protect her always. Amazingly this worked wonders for me and it was like for the first time ever I had released a pressure valve inside me.

The protection mode is now like a built-in system to me to always protect my family and friends. I did not know what my purpose in life was, especially as a young child growing up under these extreme conditions, but I have come to learn that there was a purpose in life for me at that time and a lesson in life for me during that time—to get me to where I am today.

It has taken me many years to learn how to forgive. Forgiveness is the only way to heal childhood trauma. It's the hardest thing I have ever done and will be the hardest thing you ever do.

As an adult, I went to the grave sites of my parents to talk to them both, and say out loud, "I forgive you."

This was the only way I could move forward. I grew to understand that holding onto what my childhood had been was only making me dark and angry internally.

I understand now why I am Mother to so many I meet and how this mothering instinct is a distinct quality of my leadership!

I often wondered why I was put in the family I was in. Why didn't I have happy childhood memories? Liz as an adult now is understanding why. My faith is in Jesus and I thank him for keeping me safe, for giving me the strength to be Mum to so many, for the knowledge I learnt as a struggling lost, and I felt unloved child, having to act the role of protective mother. I am aware that I can use my love to help others heal, and I thank Jesus for this. But, it all started with forgiveness. Forgiveness is not an easy task.

The Babies: My Life's Truest Blessing

At age 26 I became pregnant. Yes. To my mother, a strong Catholic, my unmarried status was shameful. I didn't feel any shame, I felt joy. I didn't care that I would have to do this alone. I felt strong and believed in myself. I was blessed. Her name is Bianca. I call her my Little Ray of Sunshine and no song could have been more perfect for her.

Bianca is my rock and I could not have done things, gone through life, reeducated myself, if it was not for her. At the drop of a hat, my beautiful daughter comes to my aid. My Little Ray of Sunshine is my strength.

At age 32 I became pregnant again. The man of my dreams was born—my most amazingly good-looking son. My heart was full. Simon has been and will always be my son, but more so the man in my life. He is my protector and guardian angel, in the distance, always watching over his mother with love.

Many more times than I can recall, I have been called upon to be a mother (mum) to friends, my children's friends, and people I meet on Facebook. Being and feeling so unloved by my Mum created doubt in my mind that I could be a good Mum to anyone, but the love letters arrived just in time.

Defining my Purpose: The Love Letters

This love note came from Bianca to help me understand why I am mother to so many and why so many come to me for mothering.

"You're not just my mum, you are everybody's mum. Nurturer, provider, carer. Without any prejudice, you take anyone in, help, listen, understand their struggles, open and non-biased."

This love note is from Anna, a dear friend who is there always even when long times have passed.

"To a woman who, through thick and thin, is there if you need her. We all now come to ask the wisdom of a well-rounded accepting mature woman with the biggest unjudging heart. We cry, we laugh, we miss periods of time but pick up again without missing a beat, but most of all her love is true."

This love note is from Coco Soliman, my friend and soul mate.

"They say in your life your soul mate appears in many forms whether it's your friend, your son, your daughter, a stranger you meet. The only way I can describe Lizzie, my dear friend of 36 years, is just that—my soul mate.

Despite all her own challenges in life, she has stood beside me and so many other people who have come into her life. She has helped guide them on their journeys in life. But even the strong can become weakened. Liz once asked me why everyone turns to her with their issues and problems, which seems to be her entire life.

My answer to her is that she has been given the role of Mothering. The mothering role is to heal people and help them on the next journey in their lives whether on earth or in spirit.

Liz has many times been my tower of strength for me and my family. I have met thousands of people over my life span, but Liz will be there until the end. I love you Liz and you are my blessing in life my dear friend."

This love note is from Victoria Cruz:

"As soon as I met Aunty Liz, I felt protected and knew I'd never be alone. In 2011, I sadly lost my son in a terrible drowning accident and my life as I knew it stopped. I found myself in a dark place with no hope and no light...and there she was, with her beaming smile and glimmer of hope, my rescuer.

Aunty Liz. She took me in, loved me, cared for me, listened to me when I needed her, and got me back on my feet. She helped me stand when I couldn't find the strength, she made me laugh at moments I wanted to cry, and made me see that although my precious boy was no longer with me, my life still needed to go on, not only for my little angel but for myself as well.

In 2014, I was blessed yet again. I had found my strength, had a loving family and home, and I awaited the arrival of a new baby boy. Once again, my hero and savior Aunty Liz, was there by my side. My son (now three) and I are so thankful for a woman who is so loving, caring, understanding, and warm, who not only gave me hope, but saved my life."

Leadership through Love has been my story!

I am humbled and blessed to receive these love notes and others I have over the years. These are not for my ego, or to impress or feel validity. These love notes are here to show me that through the darkest moments of my life, not knowing why, not understanding the lessons, not understanding the magnified hurt I felt, I finally came to believe I have a guardian angel watching over me every moment.

With my Creator knowing my purpose, as a middle-aged woman I now don't question why I am mum to all. This was my lesson, not a burden, a blessing and a gift from God.

My Truest Source of Empowerment

Through my life people have opened to me. I am trusted with their inner most secrets whether they come to ask for general help or to put a roof over their head. I now know God has put them into my life for the time that is needed, then he removes them. I know that for everyone I have helped, they have also helped me. As they move forward with more knowledge and fulfilment, service to them has enabled me to heal myself one step at a time and this brings me closer to who I want to be and who I will be tomorrow.

Only through Forgiveness.

AUTHOR ELIZABETH HASSAN

Elizabeth Hassan (Liz) is a full time Professional AIN (Assistant in Nursing) currently working as a Personal Carer. As an AIN, she has extensive experience with professionals in the mental health, physical health, legal, hospice, mediation, suicide, drug, palliative, and family communication areas. In addition, she has previous experience as a legal secretary, personal office assistant to a CEO, and a property manager.

Liz is passionate about caring for people. She acts on her skills, expertise and passion by dedicating her life to the service of others mental, physical, and spiritual well-being.

Liz cares deeply for the life of others, she feels blessed that through her experience with social media she found deep connection, relief from her isolation, and common ground with other like-minded women. This connection allowed her story, *Caring for Sara*h to be born. A story of hope, strength, and love, Liz is continuing the story of the journey *Caring for Sara* has become. A second book is in the works to relate how this one short life impacted many others, including Liz herself, even to the point of Liz having boarded a plane to take her first ever, by-her-self international flight to share a time of remembrance with Sarah's family in Europe.

Liz has lived her entire life in Melbourne Victoria, and Gold Coast Queensland, Australia. She is a mother, grandmother and loves water and nature. In addition to the second edition of *Caring for Sarah*, she is writing a book about how personal childhood struggles are often the blessings that bring forth our diamonds.

Connect with the Author. . .

Social Media

Facebook @Elizabeth Hassan (Liz Doyle)

Author Page: https://www.facebook.com/writerelizabethhassan/

"Living an Authentic and Empowered Life from the Place of Deep Self-Love and Purpose." ~ Michelle Molotte

How I Shifted Perspective and Stopped Sabotaging My Experience

THE ESSENCE OF SELF-LOVE HEALS WOUNDS OF SELF-SABOTAGE

MICHELLE MOLOTTE

As young girls, we are shown how we are supposed to act. How we are supposed to be. How we are supposed to dress, look, talk, walk, and what we are supposed to do when we grow up. Yes, men too but that's not what this chapter is about. We are taught when it's appropriate to speak up and when we must take the word of a complete stranger as having more value than our own.

Think about all the girl metaphors; she's so sweet, she looks like an angel, what a doll. I'm sure you can think of many others. We are even shamed for our womanhood—menstruation, body developments. We are taught we must not act a certain way, dress a certain way because it'll bring attention to us, usually from the boys/men. When we speak up, speak our truth, we are labeled as bitches. We are told in many ways that our voice doesn't matter.

Seeing the pendulum swing over the past decades of women's rights, many women have embraced the masculine side of business and life and turned toward a hard core- must push forward- must fight for my rights attitude. These women are making a difference at the expense of their feminine energy. I am seeing many smart and beautiful women give up their power, look the other way when it comes to being of power. This is what I call self-sabotage.

Self-sabotage comes in different shapes, forms, thoughts, feelings, actions, sizes, and habits. Most people don't think about how self-sabotaging their habits could be. I'm not talking about the normalized habits that our society talks about, I'm talking about habits that could have you experience one or more of the following:

- Depression,
- Fatigue,
- Disappointment,
- Settling for less,
- Despair,
- Dissatisfaction,
- Feeling anxious,
- Weight gain,
- Weight loss,
- Low libido,
- Stuck in an unhealthy or abusive relationship(s),
- Degrading self-talk,
- Staying in a job that isn't right for you,

...and much more. This was the state of my life for many years. People on the outside didn't know the self-sabotage that I was going through. I wore many masks to cover the depth of the pain.

Self-Sabotaging habits can build-on each other, usually through thought-processes. Someone told you how you need to be, what you need to believe, how you need to act, what you need to do, what society expects from you, and what behaviors are acceptable or not. Of course, you believed them!

Then one day, something happens. A hint of change becomes apparent, you start to feel, know, and understand there's more or perhaps a different way for you to live. At first, it's a glimmer; you might not even be aware that you know this, deep down. You keep repeating the patterns all the while, indulging in unhealthy self-talk about how awful you are.

Then you realize you're beating yourself up with thoughts of judgment because of who you think you are: not good enough, not deserving enough, not pretty enough, too fat, too skinny, not smart enough, and so on, taking you down the rabbit hole of despair and keeping the thought cycle spinning, going deeper.

You could even know there's more to your life but you're settling, just to get by. *It's just the way it is*, or *It's just who I am*. These are common statements of self-sabotage habits that must be changed to allow your feminine power.

Feminine empowerment. I'm not talking about wearing stiletto's, short dresses or anything that society would call feminine. I'm talking about being, doing, knowing from your internal environment; your gut instinct, your intuition, your connection to who you are at a deeper level than the labels you've been wearing and living since birth.

Let me share a bit of my journey from self-sabotage to self-love. For many years I lived in a constant state of self-sabotage. I experienced many of the symptoms of self-sabotage. People on the outside didn't know what I was going through. After ending my second marriage, at the beginning of the collapse of the economy in 2008, I spiraled down that rabbit hole. This created financial despair. Negative self-talk and unhealthy choices in many areas of my life. I ended up living in a 5th wheel trailer in an RV park. I would lay my head down on my pillow and cry myself to sleep, wondering what my life is about and how the hell did I get here. I went from living in a great house on acreage, having my horses and animals with me, to living in the trailer with my bank account only having $2.45 in it.

I had hit rock bottom! This was not the lifestyle I wanted! I didn't like my life. I had to change the direction I was heading, and quickly.

I started meditating and working with some of the self-help tools I had learned over the years. I was dedicated to loving myself and pulling myself up, living the way I knew I was meant to be living.

Gradually, I was shown five keys to self-love that have changed my life. I started implementing these core keys in my life and as a result; I am living in a wonderful house, on acreage and yep, my horse is right outside my window! Also, I have built a couple of successful businesses along the way and it just keeps getting better! Oh, how good it is to be living the Self-Love way of life, living in my feminine power, leading my life according to my own design!

Key #1: Compassion

What does the compassion key look like? Notice your self-talk. Stop the talk (thought). Offer yourself a positive way to see the situation. Yes, even if you are caught up in the spiral, there's ALWAYS a positive aspect to notice. It might be only a bit more positive than the original talk but it's still in the positive direction. The next time, it'll be even more positive, and so on. When you fail to stop the talk, notice it and offer yourself compassion! See, even noticing that you didn't implement the compassion key when you were triggered, is offering compassion to yourself. Have compassion for where you are in life, even when you've hit rock bottom. Pay attention to what you'd like your life to look like, instead of adding to your current situation.

How do you talk to yourself? Are you putting yourself down? Are you putting others down? Are you noticing that you want to do or say something but fear has kept you from taking action? Are you saying things to yourself like, "you're such an idiot," "you don't know what you're saying," "who would even listen to me These are a few examples of areas where you are not implementing compassion for yourself. So, pay attention to your thoughts and your words. Are they supportive or downgrading? Do they offer you a solution for what's troubling you or do they amplify the trouble? What do you say and do when someone or something triggers you? Be mindful of what you say about yourself and how you might blame others.

When you experience stressors, take a deep breath, notice your go to response. Breathe. Decide how you'd like to react. Look for a solution and then react with compassion for self. How would you talk with a friend who was experiencing the same self-sabotage patterns? Be your own friend and offer the same compassion you would to a friend!

Key #2: Be Curious

With the Curious Key, start to understand why things are the way they are for you. What role have you been playing in your life to be self-sabotaging instead of self-loving? What learned belief systems have you been playing over and over again that don't correlate with who you are? What area of your life feels out of balance? Are you living by someone else's rules? Do you perform the same behaviors and routines day in and day out? Where does this routine come from? If you self-sabotage with thoughts of judgment, where did that judgment come from? Is it serving you for your highest good? Probably not!

Be curious. Why are you triggered? Be curious why this person or event has upset you. It starts with your belief systems. Your past programming.

Be curious. Where did this program come from? Be curious. Is there a different way you could be conducting yourself if you had a choice to choose a different reaction?

Be curious. You could ask yourself why you do what you do and with the curious side of you, with compassion, try on a new behavior, outlook, and action!

To be curious about any part of your life that is out of balance is a crucial step to go from self-sabotage to self-love.

Once you start looking with curiosity, you may find it enlightening, fun, and life changing.

Key #3: Laugh

Laugh at your negative thoughts. Laugh at your negative words. Laugh at your mistakes. Laugh at your judgment towards yourself and others. You choose how you react! When you find yourself caught up in the self-sabotage, laugh!

Go ahead, try it! Ok, you might not be able to pull up a full belly laugh at this point, try a giggle. If that doesn't work, SMILE! Even a slight smile.

Did you notice a shift within your body? A relaxation of your shoulder. A release of your breath. A small flutter in your stomach? If not, that's ok; eventually it'll turn into a full-on laugh if you remain aware of the opportunities to replace the negative with laughter.

With this Key, you'll not only affect your mind and emotions, you'll experience a physical effect within your body. You will be releasing your happy chemicals. When you laugh, your cells get a wonderful dose of Dopamine, Serotonin, Oxytocin, and Endorphins! These chemicals are your feel-good chemicals.

You can't be experiencing your feel-good chemicals and feel-bad chemicals at the same time. When you laugh, you are allowing your body to de-stress, even if it's for a minute. When you de-stress, you are able to think clearer, notice your thinking, and then allow for all five keys to transform the self-sabotaging habit you're getting to laugh at! This may feel weird at first but it is such an amazing way to look at triggers and to be fully present within your body and in the situation.

Key #4: Truth

Speaking your Truth. Knowing your Truth. Trusting your Truth. If you are not speaking your truth, you are engaging in the self-sabotage habit. If you aren't telling yourself the truth, you are foregoing self-love. Speaking your needs, wants, desires, likes, and dislikes to yourself and others is imperative on the path to self-love. You might not want to hurt another's feelings by speaking what you want. You might not want to do something and go along with it to avoid conflict, therefore, not speaking your truth. Maybe you tell someone that you'll do something and then dread that you had agreed to it. Or you say, "all is good," "everything's fine," "that's OK," all the while you are steaming inside because you feel disrespected, unheard, or even unseen.

This assures that your needs will go unmet. That is not OK! Your needs, wants, and desires are as important as the next person's. Who wants to live life fulfilling everyone else's desires and putting their own aside? Many people do, and at what cost: depression, fatigue, feeling worthless, unloved, and low self-esteem. Not speaking your truth can have detrimental effects on the body and the psyche.

First step for this key is to start telling yourself the truth. Notice when you really want to say yes but you say no or vice versa. Just notice. Make note how your body feels. Notice the thoughts that swirl in your head afterwards. Tell yourself what you would have rather wanted to say and then let it go. Don't perseverate when you have declined to speak your truth. Noticing is the best first step!

Once you notice the times when you aren't speaking up, it's time to speak up. Start small. You can start with a trusted friend or family member. Check in with yourself before agreeing to something. Notice what you'd really like say and do and then share your truth. See how that feels for you. Yes, the other person might not like it and that's OK. What's important is you are OK within! Yes, it does take practice and learning to trust you. It can be done! You are worth it!

Key #5: QTIP—Quit Taking It Personally!

It might be, to some, easier said than done, yet it is a life changing concept and it's really an important one to focus on.

Do you easily get upset, cry, get angry, storm off, or shut down when someone says or does something that, in your perspective, is wrong or you don't like it?

Do you continue to relive the event over and over, in your mind?

Do you gossip, complain or blame somebody else for what they have done to you or said to you or said about you?

If you've answered yes to any of these questions, then you are taking it personally. You are allowing someone else's words and actions to have more meaning and truth than your own inner knowing and your own truth. See, when someone else is directing their words at you, that's just what it is: their words, their perspective, their vocabulary, their meaning. It's up to you to choose the label you put on them. Yes, someone may be angry at you but it's your choice how you let those words affect you. You can take it personally and lose control, step into the self-sabotage habit, stress your body and your emotions. Or, you can take that deep breath, and remind yourself that it's not yours to take personally.

Hear what the other person is saying. Acknowledge what they said could be their truth, but do not take it personally! You could learn from what they are saying or doing, just do not take it personally!

Do you see how all five keys play a role in moving from the self-sabotage habit to the self-love habit? I learned that I am the only one in control of my own thoughts, beliefs, patterns, feelings and behaviors. Because of knowing how I didn't want to be living my life, I took charge and learned to lead from my feminine power. Self-love.

AUTHOR MICHELLE MOLOTTE

Michelle Molotte, speaker, author, trainer, coach, hand analyst and intuitive. Michelle's passion and purpose is to lead women into their own individual power, cultivating their purpose and living their life according to their inner desire, their purpose. Michelle has spoken at small, intimate, women's events and on stages for government departments and businesses. She is a lover of learning, dance, animals and supporting people on their journey. Currently, Michelle lives in Oregon with visions of big adventures.

I dedicate this chapter to my two children, Chelsea and Austin, for loving me through it all.

Connect with the Author. . .

Website: www.michellemolotte.com
Email: michelle@michellemolotte.com

CHAPTER 17

"Wisdom comes in whispers." ~ *Joy S. Pedersen*

Leadership with Love

JOY S. PEDERSEN

*A*s the cause of darkness has been cleared leaving God back in charge of the planet, much will begin to change as we edge into the next golden age.

The world has been run by darkness for so long, people don't likely even know the difference as to when God is really in charge. Because people have given their power over to the darkness for so long, those in leadership positions to date have sometimes unknowingly perpetuated the manipulation of darkness.

The real leaders behind the scenes have been undermining the possibilities available to humanity. As people begin to recognize the difference between the light and the dark forces, they can begin taking their power back to use for more effective outcomes.

Why did I title this chapter, *Leadership with Love*? I received the following message from God on the future of business.

"Love must be at the core of all business. Why do I say love? Because I am love. That is who I am. I am love. When you are aligned with Me, you are in love. When you love your work, you are aligned with Me and it becomes an easy workflow. Deadlines are met much easier.

All the resources you require will be at your fingertips. You will lack for nothing. You will enjoy what you do and want to do more of it but you will be guided as to when to work and when not to when to play and when not to."

When you choose to align with God within, whom you access through your heart, you are connected to the greatest love and source of all. You can then tap into that resource and gain the assistance of the most powerful you can lead with love.

In my practice as a spiritual healer, I work with leaders and business owners on a weekly basis. The goal is to help them let go of the limited beliefs and fears that are ultimately shadowing the results they can achieve. When someone operates from their subconscious, the part of you that manifests results, the state of which you exist matters substantially. If trying to lead your own life, or the lives and efforts of others effectively, you need to have clarity of thought and purpose.

Decisions need to be made with the whole in mind and not just from a place of win/lose, which was often the leadership in the past. If making a fear-based decision, results will be created out of imbalance.

As God also said, "Humanity's way of doing business today has enslaved you to technology, to the desk, and to a business. People are to no longer be enslaved by anyone or anything. Herein I state one of the dictates of this new world. No one is to be enslaved by an idea, by a person, by a tradition, by anyone, or by anything. No one is to be enslaved. To do so, would be causing grave harm. It is not for you or anyone to cause harm."

Humanity must be trained as to how to do business in this new world. God also said, "The future of business is not about you doing. It will be about you being. My way of doing business is not the way you have been used to so far. You will find dramatic differences in the way I do business versus the way humanity does business."

"I recommend letting go of your attachments to the way humanity has done business so far. The way humanity has done business so far has limited its ability to create divinely and what is divinely possible.

What has occurred in the past has been based on limited thinking. Humanity's way of doing business is based on limited thinking, lack, greed, control, manipulation. It has not been created in balance."

So, how does this affect the leaders of today? We can't lead from the old paradigm. We must be able to tap into the Source of all to be guided according to the big picture, divine purpose, and with the whole in mind. But changing from old programming and previous methods of doing business to what God has in mind comes with its own challenges. We are so used to being controlled and lead with an iron fist that we don't even recognize the freedom we have by aligning with God within. We have been aligned with the leaders who have programmed our minds for limitation, lack, and fear. Of course, there are those in leadership positions, such as motivators, trying to empower us, but they, too, are limited often from their programming and humanity's way of doing things. They may not be aware of God's way of doing things.

I have found God's way is more in the moment, living out of divine inspiration with great purpose in mind. Many forms of leadership are restricted to doing things in a productive manner. It may be according to a particular philosophy perpetuated from the intellect with good intentions. What if you can be inspired by God to do things beyond the imaginable?

Following humanity's way of doing things versus God's way of doing things is vastly different. Humanity's way is living out of the past, repeating what has been experienced in the past and established as possible best practices. God's way is taking into consideration all possible scenarios and not necessarily based only on past experience. His view is vast and His resources limitless.

By tapping into that energy, being guided by the divine in the moment, without always knowing the end result nor why, you may find yourself ending up in places beyond the imagination.

So, as a leader, do you want to lead from the past or from the infinite? Do you want to lead out of humanity's way of doing things or

God's way of doing things? Which do you feel holds more possibility for you? Which is more comfortable?

If you want to lead as part of the new reality, letting go of the past is key. Releasing limiting beliefs and old programming is necessary if you want to excel in this new world of infinite possibility. As an intuitive, I can tune into the subconscious mind, the memory bank and computer, and identify the hidden causes of someone's challenges. Using spiritual healing gifts, I release the cause of those discoveries.

I work over the phone with my eyes closed, tuning into the client's energy and subconscious. Over the years, I have discovered issues that have contributed to common challenges experienced today. These common denominators are limiting people and their power. I clear power in general and all times someone has been powerful and misused their power as well as times their power has been diminished. All times those in leadership positions have taken their power has often caused them to fear power and also fear to not want to become that kind of leader. Until they release old memories of issues around power, they aren't capable of fully becoming the leader that they could this lifetime.

Another common area I clear is rules created and forced upon humanity from governments, religions, institutions, and society. Many are limited in their ability to fully self-express until they release those negative memories and subconscious fears of not following the rules out of fear of persecution and oppression. How many lifetimes have we lived suffering from oppression while living up to someone else's expectations?

The world has largely been win/lose with the few elite running the show inhibiting the freedoms of the majority.

The subconscious is the part of us that manifests our results. It is the subconscious that must be cleared of the limited beliefs and fears, programming, and patterns that are generating and attracting the results out of the hidden mindset operating behind the scenes.

If someone wants to be an effective and a fully expressed leader, they must be free of their negative memories that are holding them back and coloring their perspectives, experiences, and outcomes. By setting the client free, the client can then become the leader they are meant to be.

An effective leader is one who is free of baggage, and can stand fearlessly in their own power. By being aligned with the divine within one's own heart, they can move forward effortlessly accomplishing that which is divinely guided and supported.

Everyone here on this planet came with the ideal resources, looks, inspirations, and desires to achieve what is purposeful for them in this lifetime. By removing the blocks to experiencing this life in its fullness, that purpose can be fulfilled more easily. So much baggage influences and interrupts possibilities. Releasing the old and outmoded thought patterns frees the individual to express themselves and allows God to work through them.

People don't often realize how much they block God. People know how often they have turned away from God on a daily basis while trying to find their way in the world. Turning away, combined often with religious teachings that have created fear of God, hasn't helped. The guilt of separating and turning away from God, along with the fear of God, often blocks God from giving to the person because they are blocked from receiving.

Fortunately, we can clear those issues setting people free from those blocks to receiving from and being divinely guided by God. Once free of blocks, the person soars and can lead more easily and eloquently. They can be fully supported by God and his team of ascended masters, angels, and archangels, all available to support the leader to more effortlessly succeed in their path of service.

Can you imagine being inspired and powered by God to serve as guided while provided the resources to succeed most easily?

How encouraging would it be to be on purpose, fully supported by Heaven, doing what is most purposeful, making the difference you were meant to make this lifetime?

By letting go of the past, you more easily change the future. By aligning with God, there are no limitations as to your success. You will do what is meant for you and the audience you were meant to lead.

And, no matter who you were meant to lead, whether it a family or an empire, you will make the biggest difference because of being fully empowered by God leading as directed with the highest and best good in mind for all. And, you will enjoy the feeling of being fully self-expressed, living on purpose, and fulfilling your mission here on Earth.

When you are inspired, you more easily inspire others. The impact you can make fully self-expressed, when empowered and inspired is a wonderful combination.

When you lead from the heart while connected to and inspired by God, you lead people to what is infinitely possible for them. But, you can only lead people where you have been able to go. So, your work on yourself to let go and be fully expressed is paramount. When true to yourself and your calling, you will be a significant door opener to those you were meant to lead and inspire.

Life is short. The quicker you are able to realize and express your gifts, allowing God to power your process, the bigger impact you will make. Leading as appropriate and serving whom appropriate in the ideal way for their needs is the perfect formula for a successful leader.

May you lead with heart and grace impacting the world with your gifts in your unique way.

AUTHOR JOY S. PEDERSEN, D.D., L.S.H., C.S.H.C.

Joy S. Pedersen is an international best-selling author, Doctor of Divinity, Licensed Spiritual Healer and Certified Spiritual Health Coach. As Founder and President of Express Success LLC, she serves a primarily international business and professional clientele helping them identify and clear the cause of their personal and business challenges. You can read more about her work at www.JoyPedersen.com and can receive gifts at www.GiftsFromJoy.com that further elaborates on the unique concepts of her work.

Connect with the Author. . .

Website

Http://www.JoyPedersen.com

http://www.giftsfromjoy.com

Social Media

Facebook: https://www.facebook.com/drjoypedersen

Twitter: http://www.twitter.com/joypedersen

"A Leader has a clear vision and can communicate and share that vision. Leaders are able to communicate their vision clearly so that others see the vision and want to journey with that leader to the destination." ~ *Trish Springsteen*

Speak for Success as a Leader
Solve the Leadership Puzzle

TRISH SPRINGSTEEN

*L*eader. It is a simple word. We know the meaning of leader as being a person we follow. Or do we?

When I speak to people about leaders. I ask, "What does being a leader mean to you?"

In their answers, I discover that leadership is more complex than a simple dictionary definition. I can ask five different people and receive five different answers. Right here in this book you will discover different meanings of leader in each chapter that you read.

There is one basic concept that all leaders must have: Followers. You can't lead without followers. Followers may be obvious (e.g., teams, defense force personnel, corporate staff), or they may be subtle (e.g., your mum, your dad, your parents). Any person you look up to for guidance is a leader. Many lead by example and may not even be aware of their followers.

When the definition of leadership includes knowing that followers are in the mix, there is one important element that becomes apparent and one that is often missed, forgotten, or badly used. That is communication. The successful leader is one who has good speaking and communication skills.

To lead people, you must communicate your vision, your mission, and your instructions. Being able to do so is the distinguishing factor between bad leaders, good leaders, and effective leaders.

These concepts make sense to me. I know how important speaking and communication skills have been to my success as a leader.

Over the years I have seen and been on the wrong end of poor leadership due to lack of communication and poor speaking skills. I've been in jobs where credibility, time, and productivity were lost because team leaders and managers could not give clear directions or even get us to buy into the vision and mission of the organization.

I am relieved to note that whenever theory of leadership is discussed, it is agreed that the central requirement of leaders is to provide direction, to outline the vision, and point the organization in the direction it needs to go. The vision and direction remains the responsibility of the leader to define and communicate.

"The art of Communication is the Language of Leadership."

~ James Humes

As a leader, you must sell your vision to your followers. A leader convinces followers to buy into the vision, adopt it for their own, and commit to the pathway that the leader sees them travelling. Before the leader can do this, they must clearly understand where they are going and to structure a clear message to convey this. It requires strong word skills as well as persuasive presentation skills and an ability to communicate in a clear manner.

To bring followers on the journey, the leader must get commitment to the vision and mission, on both the intellectual level and the emotional level. In addition to the strong communication skills already noted, reaching followers emotionally and intellectually requires charisma and a passionate connection with the concept and message. Add in great body language and vocal variety when connecting with their followers and you have a leader who is successful.

It is easy to see that communication and leadership are closely bound. Books about leadership, as well as reports and statistics, advise that poor quality or lack of communication is considered among the top three issues that lead to failure in leadership, as identified by leaders and managers.

What many forget is that communication is a two-way process involving speaking (transmitting) plus listening (receiving). To be a better, more confident communicator and a successful leader, develop your listening skills. Listen to your staff, to your team, to others in your organization, to the public, and to your own leaders. Emulate their listening styles. Be aware of what is going on around you. Be alert to opportunities to foster development of the great team.

Listen carefully. This will help you identify areas that need attention and to see opportunities for improvement that arise. From my experience as a leader, I have certainly found cultivating my listening skills always helps me to connect with my teams.

What I find confuses many followers and new leaders alike is the variety and number of different leadership styles emerging. There are servant leaders, situational leaders, laissez–faire leaders, charismatic leaders, autocratic leaders, transformational leaders, and democratic leaders. The list continues to grow. It seems to me that there is a new leadership style every time I turn around.

It is confusing, and I recently found myself questioning my own preferred leadership style. Does my style of leadership impact on how good a leader I am? If so, how do I choose which style is best? Which style fits my personality and experience? Which best fits the needs of my followers?

After researching and trying out different leadership styles, reading books, speaking to other leaders, their teams, and staff, I found that the type of Leadership you adopt is indicated by your answer to one simple question; which is:

"In these circumstances, in this time frame and with this team and resources—how much input am I going to allow my team into the decision-making process?"

There are three possible answers:

- None
- Some
- All

A leader who chooses *None* is an Authoritarian leader who decides what is to be done, who is going to do it, and even how it should be done. Authoritarian leadership style is effective in times of crisis where the team looks for decisive leadership and expects control and command. Followers will respect the leader for taking immediate action.

A leader who answers *Some* uses an Inclusive type of leadership; where the input of the team is important and valued. It is also known as Democratic or Participative. Basically, it means that the leader seeks consensus because followers identify far more with practices designed by themselves for agreed outcomes.

When followers are experienced and qualified to handle tasks without a leader breathing down their necks, the Laissez-faire type of Leadership is the likely choice. Give this type of team the task, the resources, and the time frame—then leave them to complete the project. a good leader will maintain a watch—after all the responsibility does rest with the leader—and delegate with confidence. It takes an experienced team with a strong leader to make this leadership style work. It also takes a good relationship built on trust and confidence.

The most obvious choice for many leaders is either Authoritarian or Inclusive.

What I found was that as I simplified my choice of leadership style, it was easier to choose the effective communication style to go with that leadership style.

There are two types of communication: Directive (straight forward, to the point, do this—do that) and Connective (based more in relationship building—we did this together).

Directive communication works best with authoritarian leadership and connective with inclusive and laissez-fair leadership. If you think about these two communication styles, you will also see that in general directive communication is a male default and connective communication is a female default. This becomes important when we look at female leadership.

It was something I realized early in my leadership forays. Often, I was not taken seriously in the boardroom. I was dismissed by my fellow male leaders. I sat back and analyzed my leadership style and then looked at my communication style.

My communication was connective, which worked well with my team, and not so well when I wanted to be noticed amongst my peers. I changed my style to reflect the playing field. In the boardroom, when I wanted to be noticed and have my leadership acknowledged, I became direct—this is what I did on the project, then I backed it up and included my team members' input.

Previously I would start with, "My team did this," and then explain how I directed. By the time I got to what I did, I lost the attention and focus of the other leaders. It's all about knowing your leadership style and when to use it, and your communication style and when to use it.

It's about believing in yourself as a leader, believing in your expertise. Act by knowing what your vision is, what your message, is and then use great communication and speaking skills to share that vision and mission with your followers to take them on the journey with you.

I have been in leadership roles in male dominated fields, such as medical indemnity and energy; in volunteer organizations at various levels; in my business with my team and my clients and as an influencer with followers who see me as a mentor and a role model.

When you put the leadership puzzle together, it looks like this:

1. Clarity—knowing where you are going, what your vision and message is

2. Belief—in yourself as a leader, in your expertise and knowledge

3. Trust—in yourself and in your team and/or followers

4. Confidence—to share your vision and mission and take your followers on a journey

5. Speaking and Communication Skills—to share, clearly your message and vision engaging both the intellectual content and the emotional connections

6. The Leadership Question—to determine your leadership style

7. Directive and Connective Communication—matching your communication to your leadership, the outcome you want to achieve and the situation

This is the whole picture of you as a Successful Leader.

Enjoy your journey.

AUTHOR TRISH SPRINGSTEEN

Trish Springsteen is a multi-international award-winning speaker, mentor, author, and radio host who specializes in speaker training. Trish is the co-founder and owner of Trischel, a company dedicated to bringing communication and effective speaking skills to individuals, businesses, and organizations.

Trish has spoken on national and international stages and she is passionate about creating confident communicators.

Trish believes her mantra, Believe ~ Act ~ Share, enables her to deliver a message of empowerment that provides the building blocks and the foundation for Success. From personal experience Trish knows the key to success as a leader is to clearly communicate your vision and message. Speaking skills are a vital ingredient to that success.

Trish is the Gold Winner in the 2016 Women World Awards Woman of the Year - Mentor or Coach of the Year and Bronze Winner in the 2016 Women World Awards Female Entrepreneur of the Year and won the National Edupreneur 2015 Award in the Professional Speaking Category. In addition, Trish was a Finalist in the 2016 Australian Small Business Champion Awards and a Finalist in the ILAB Global Impact 2015 Awards.

Trish is the author of Creating Confident Communicators co-author and contributing author of 8 other books including: The Book of Success, Every Entrepreneurs Guide: Running your Own Business, Women on a Mission, and The Book of Inspiration for Women by Women

---

Connect with the Author. . .

Website
www.trishspringsteen.com
www.trischel.com.au

Social Media
LinkedIn: http://www.linkedin.com/in/trishspringsteen/
Twitter: @TrishatTrischel
Facebook: https://www.facebook.com/Trischel https://www.facebook.com/trishspringsteenspeaking
YouTube: TrischelBrisbane Channel: http://bit.ly/TrishTalks
Instagram: https://www.instagram.com/trishspringsteen/
Email: info@trischel.com.au

Author Pages
Goodreads: https://www.goodreads.com/author/show/13480197.Trish_Springsteen
Amazon: https://www.amazon.com/Trish-Springsteen/e/B01GMA-DID2

"Leadership is having the ability to provide a space where people can develop their creativity, stretch their boundaries, and accomplish their goals in a way that's true to their authentic self." ~ Gloria Grace Rand

Reluctant Leader No More

STEPPING OUT OF THE SHADOWS AND INTO THE SPOTLIGHT

GLORIA GRACE RAND

I AM a leader.
I always have been a leader. It's only been in the last year that I have fully embraced that role. Before that, I called myself a reluctant leader. But that was just a story I told myself. It wasn't based in reality. Quite the contrary. I've been a leader since I was a child. I've only come to terms with this realization in the last year. It happened thanks to my participation in a mastermind group, appropriately called *Lead*.

So where did this faulty story come from? And how did I come to write a new story? Let's start at the beginning to give you context.

I grew up in the 1960s, in a suburb of Detroit, Michigan. I was the baby of the family. My sister was 10 years older than me, and my brother was 14 years older.

My dad was an alcoholic and my mother was prone to depression and fits of rage. Not a recipe for a happy marriage, let alone a picture-perfect childhood.

But despite that upbringing, or maybe because of it, I embraced leadership at school, and later as a young adult. It was only after I became a parent myself that my perspective shifted. I became more reluctant about being a leader. But I'm getting ahead of myself.

The Precocious Leader

One of the first memories I have of leading was prompted by a discussion with one of my best friends. We had been talking about how long we'd known each other. She told me her earliest memory of me was in Kindergarten, when I sat at the front of the room and read a story to the entire class.

There were other times when I chose to be a leader. I had attended Girl Scout camp every summer since I was seven years old. So, as a teenager, it seemed only natural to me to become a Counselor in Training. I got to lead a group of 9-year-old girls, (under supervision), which was a lot of fun.

Back at school, I auditioned and won the chance to conduct our school band for one number during a spring concert.

After I graduated from college and moved to Florida, I joined the choir at church and teamed up with another choir member to organize social events for the group. I even wrote a *Choir Notes* newsletter—foreshadowing a service I would later offer clients as part of my copywriting business.

I undertook several leadership roles during my professional career that began when I was employed by the PBS TV news program, *Nightly Business Report*. My first job with NBR involved training the newsroom staff on the new computer system.

NBR was a great place to work because my bosses encouraged me to learn new skills. As staff members left to pursue other jobs, I took on their positions. I served as stocks producer, associate producer/writer, and filled in occasionally as graphics producer. Eventually, I assumed the role of backup producer, filling in for the senior producer of the program whenever she was away.

Talk about responsibility! I was in charge of a program that aired live on 240+ public television stations across the United States. I assigned stories, wrote and edited scripts, and timed the broadcast from the control room.

Managing the show's timing was no easy feat because the broadcast included live interviews and an unscripted stock segment that the late, great co-anchor Paul Kangas delivered each night. It was exciting and challenging work, and I loved it.

My employment at NBR coincided with major developments in my personal life too. I got married and started a family, giving birth to a daughter and then, two years later, a son.

The Reluctant Leader Appears

This reluctant leader notion first showed up when my daughter was seven years old.

I wanted her to be a Girl Scout like I had been. When the opportunity came for her to be a Brownie, I went to a sign-up meeting. The woman in charge said the only way a troop could be formed was if someone volunteered to be a leader.

A hush fell over the crowd.

(Forgive me... I've always wanted to use that phrase.)

Really, there were a few minutes of awkward silence as all the women in the room, including me, looked around at each other, to see who would raise their hand and say, "Yes, I'll do it."

I didn't want my daughter to miss out on what was one of the best experiences I had growing up. So I volunteered. While I was reluctant at first, it turned out to be a rewarding experience. As leadership often does, come to think of it!

The girls in our troop were awesome. I had fun coming up with activities for them to do, and fun watching them learn, play and grow together. It was a lot of work at times—especially during Girl Scout Cookie season—but I'm glad I stepped up to the plate and took the leadership reins. And I'm proud that I could be a role model for my daughter and the other girls in the troop.

I reluctantly took on another leadership role around the same time—becoming co-president of the Parent Teacher Organization at my children's school. I didn't want the entire responsibility falling on my shoulders, but I was willing to be part of a team.

After I left NBR and started my own business, I struggled with leadership again. Successful business owners know there comes a time when you must hire people to grow. I didn't know how to delegate. And to be honest, I wasn't sure I could trust someone to handle certain tasks as well I could. As a result, the first assistant I hired did not work out. But it wasn't her fault. I had no systems in place for her to handle, and I had not set up ground rules for how we would communicate with each other. Thankfully, I learned from that experience. The next person I hired worked out much better.

Buying into the Superwoman Myth

Looking back on it, I believe this reluctant leader attitude stems from the fact that I had unconsciously embraced the crazy notion that I had to be a superwoman and excel at everything. Can you relate?

I put pressure on myself because I wanted to give my kids a better childhood than the one I received. I conveniently forgot that my kids were already ahead of the game because my husband was not an alcoholic. He was a loving dad. And when I occasionally lost my temper, I apologized. Something my mother never did.

As a business owner, I would go above and beyond for my clients. Then, I'd grow frustrated that I wasn't making as much money as I thought I should be, or as I saw others doing. My sister, God bless her, would remind me that I was doing an awesome job, and I should give myself a break.

I willingly took on a leadership role in my business by conducting an online marketing workshop. That was a lot of work, but at the end of the two days, I wanted to do it again. I liked teaching people. Stepping back into a leadership role in that way allowed me to tap back into how I felt when I was younger.

But just when it seemed I had gotten my mojo back, life interrupted, as it tends to do. Turns out the Universe still had some lessons to teach me about leadership.

Masterminding My Way Back from the Brink

The event that rocked my world happened in July 2015. That's when my sister was diagnosed with a rare form of cancer. Since our parents and brother were deceased, and she had no children of her own, I was the only family she had to help her through this ordeal.

This was certainly not a job I wanted, nor one she wanted me to have. But it was a job I could do. I had caregiver experience, dating back to childhood. I would bring ice packs to my mom when she suffered from migraine headaches. I would massage her hands that were racked with arthritis. And I comforted her when my brother passed away suddenly at the age of 33–on Mother's Day, no less. And of course, once I became a parent, I nursed my children back to health when they were sick or injured.

Sadly, I couldn't nurse my sister back to health. The cancer was too aggressive. I was able to move in during her last months and be her primary caregiver when she was no longer able to walk on her own.

Watching someone you love succumb to cancer is no easy feat. I was fortunate to have support: my husband and children, my sister's friends and co-workers, and the hospice staff at the end of her life.

I also gained support from a group of people who became my second family during this stressful time. They were members of Lead the mastermind program I invested in so that I could learn how to run my own masterminds. This comprehensive program included business and personal development coaching, along with facilitator development training. It was through the coaching I received from the leaders of the program, and the wisdom and knowledge shared by the other members of the mastermind, that I came to understand and appreciate that I am a leader.

Struggling to run a business, and then dealing with my sister's illness had sent me into a downward spiral, shaking my self-confidence.

I had discounted my value as a leader. All the old fears and insecurities I had growing up, and the feelings of not being enough had reasserted themselves. It makes sense in retrospect because I felt out of control because I couldn't stop the cancer. I couldn't save my sister's life. Losing her meant losing the last member of the family I grew up with. That's still something I mourn.

But the Lead group helped me to see that the fears were old baggage I didn't need to hang onto any longer. This reluctant leader idea was just a story I was telling myself. The group helped me see how strong I am, how much value I provide my family, friends and clients, and that I truly am a leader. I am blessed to have had them in my life when I needed that support.

The experience confirmed for me why I want to lead my own masterminds. When you bring together a group of people who are as committed to achieving their own goals as they are to seeing the other members achieve their goals, magic happens.

I'm now comfortable in the spotlight once more—leading myself, my family and my community. The lesson I hope you'll take away is that there's no reason for you to remain in the shadows when you feel called to be a leader. Step into the spotlight and embrace that call. It's your intuition telling you that this is the right move for you to make, for yourself, your family, and your community.

AUTHOR GLORIA GRACE RAND

Gloria is an Online Visibility Strategist, award-winning SEO blogger, Certified High-Performance Speaker, and trained Mastermind Facilitator. She believes women have innate leadership qualities and we need to be confident about sharing our unique gifts with the world. Gloria facilitates masterminds for women solopreneurs to creatively bring out their authentic self online, so they gain more clients with less stress and more fun.

A former writer and producer for public television's Nightly Business Report, Gloria has been recognized as a top SEO copywriting blogger by Wordstream. She is a Contributing Author to the number one best-selling book, *Connect: 100 + Mind-Blowing Strategies to Use Social Media and Drive Business Growth* and a contributor to *Mogul Mom: How to Quit Your Job, Start Your Own Business*, and *Join the Work-at-Home Mom Revolution*. She has been a featured leading expert on Central Florida News 13 TV.

You can count on Gloria to deliver a content rich, experiential and powerful, heartfelt presentation that will change the way audiences market their businesses online. Her clients attest that after working with her, the benefits to them have been priceless.

Connect with the Author. . .

Website: http://gloriarand.com
Social Media
  Facebook: https://www.facebook.com/gloriarand
  LinkedIn: https://www.linkedin.com/in/gloriarand
  Twitter: https://twitter.com/GloriaGraceRand

"If your actions inspire others to dream more, learn more, do more, and become more, you are a leader." ~ John Quincy Adams

The Introverted Leader

How to Succeed in a Noisy, Extroverted World

VICKI IBAUGH

*T*he fact that today I am considered a leader seemed quite unlikely based on my past. You see, I was the shy girl....

Imagine a group of fourth graders sitting on the floor for reading circle with the teacher having students taking turns reading out loud. I was the one praying the teacher would not get to me, trying to make myself small and hiding behind my book.

That was my norm during elementary school; I drew myself in and tried to disappear to avoid being called on. I was not a hand raiser. I did not shout out the answers. I was both shy and an introvert and yet I was also an exceptional learner, hard worker, natural organizer, and teacher. Today I still consider myself to be an introvert who can be shy, but I also consider myself to be a successful leader.

Are you the quiet one? Do you avoid stepping forward? Are you the hard worker everyone can depend on? Are you the one who knows everything that is going on and absorbs all around you yet rarely speaks up?

You are the reason I am sharing my experience and the tools I have used over the past four decades. Too often I see women and girls dismiss being a leader because they share in my shy and introverted nature. They believe unless they are naturally outgoing and the life of the party, they can't be a leader. Sometimes, like me back in my early years, they don't think what they say matters or they fear being judged for what they say. So instead of stepping forward, they stay quiet. Too often you are the one who listens and considers all the information before formulating an opinion only to find the group has decided on a course of action without your voice being heard.

Too often our world thinks extroverts make the best leaders. I am here to challenge that myth by sharing my journey and experience. My hope is to inspire the introvert who might read this book to share her gifts and to step forward into leadership because the world needs introverted leaders too.

The key to success as an introvert is to AMP up your leadership abilities. AMP is the process I used, without initially realizing it, to move from being the little girl who wanted to disappear to being the leader of my own business, a certified speaker, best-selling author, and a chapter leader for Women's Prosperity Network (a women's networking and mastermind group). This transition started with the small steps that define the acronym AMP.

A—Accept and Acknowledge Your Energy Type and Your Strengths

It took me many years to learn that being introverted did not mean there was something wrong with me or that I needed to act like someone I wasn't. I had to learn that being shy and being introverted were NOT the same thing. Being shy is social; I was afraid to make a mistake or look foolish in a social situation. Being introverted is about where my energy comes from. You see, as an introvert my energy comes from time alone rather than being a crowd of people.

I accept that my energy comes from being alone and that there is absolutely nothing wrong with that. I also accept that I prefer to think things through before responding, a common trait among introverts. We reflect and give our thoughts time.

When faced with needing to make a choice, a strategy that has served me well is to say, "I would really like to give this some careful thought. Can I get back with you tomorrow?"

People respect that you want to think before giving an answer. Only rarely has someone not given me a yes response to this. The key is communicating your needs as they relate to your energy.

We will dive further into managing your energy in a moment. Let us now also touch on accepting your strengths. Too often we focus on what we are not good at and don't acknowledge our gifts and strengths. As an introvert, I discovered I was a great listener, writer, critical thinker, and learner. I was great in one-on-one or small groups.

Three of my biggest strengths were being organized, having lots of knowledge, and being willing and able to teach others. It is from these strengths that I was recognized by my peers, teachers, and superiors and placed into leadership roles. In fact, my first leadership role was tutoring other students which pulled directly from my strengths. As I moved into my career, I was also asked to lead training for new nurses, develop online courses programs, and to oversee policy and procedure changes.

You see rather than looking at what I was not good at, I leaned into the things I was great at doing and let them be my path for leading.

What are your strengths? What is it that you are naturally good at doing? We all have talents, gifts, and abilities. Accept and acknowledge yours and let them be your own path to leading.

M—Manage Your Energy

The biggest difference between introverts and extroverts is how we recharge our energy. Extroverts often feel drained from being alone and they recharge and energize from being around other people. Introverts are often the opposite. We are drained after being in groups of people and become recharged by spending time alone. For the longest time, I could not figure out why two days into large events I was crabby and wanting to be alone. Today I realize it was because my energy was zapped and that what I needed was time alone. While I could easily not go to large events, instead I choose to attend and plan my time to provide a balance between being with others and being alone. One of my key strategies is getting my own room. It gives me a quiet space to relax and let my energy return.

Another way I have learned to manage my energy when I need to engage with others as a speaker or in my day-to-day work is to arrange my schedule so that before and after spending time with others I keep openings in my schedule giving me time to recharge alone. The work I do often takes 100 percent of my energy. By taking this time in my schedule to recharge, it allows me to give 100 percent of myself when I am with others. Remember while extroverts gain energy in these situations, us introverts lose energy. Knowing this allows me to manage my energy dynamic, and I show up better as a leader.

Do you find interacting with people and going to events, such as meetings and networking, drains you? How can you set up your time to manage your energy?

P—Plan, Push, and Practice

This part of the AMP process is one of the hardest because it involves moving outside your comfort zone. Introverts are very happy staying in their comfort zone. Yet to grow and develop you need to learn and try new things, which can be pretty scary at first. So, the first thing I learned to do whenever I knew I needed to stretch my comfort zone was to plan.

For example, I committed to attend a 3-day speaker boot camp where I would give short presentations to complete strangers. I could have let the fear stop me, but instead I contacted the organizer and shared with her my concerns. She told me how the event itself was going to handle many of them. My plan included getting to the location early so I could get a feel for the room and the space. As I stood in the space where I would present and looked out at the room, I reminded myself I was safe and that everyone here wanted to support me in being successful. I visualized completing my presentation and feeling great!

You see sometimes to move to the next level, you will need to push past your fears and push outside your comfort zone. Doing so is scary, but not deadly. In fact, every time I have pushed my limits, I have had an overwhelming sense of pride in myself. A genuine feeling of, *I did it and it was actually not too bad.* In addition, each push has opened new doors to leadership and a new inner strength of, *I can do this.*

As with anything new, it can feel awkward and uncomfortable at first. That is where the practice piece comes into play. Remember even the expert was once a beginner. As you push into new areas, make time to keep practicing. I made sure to speak in public at least once each month and to practice as if I was in the room using my visualization technique to make it seem real. Also, because networking was another push area for me, I attended events regularly. I managed my energy before each event, planned for each, and went into the situation ready to push forward. By doing this over time, it became easier and easier. Practice does make perfect. My comfort zone kept expanding and my leadership skills have continued to grow.

What is lurking outside your comfort zone that would help you move forward? What small actions can you take to plan, push, and practice?

What's Next:

My sincere hope is that I have used my struggles and challenges to help you (or the introvert in your life) to know you are not alone and that introverts can indeed become exceptional leaders. Today, as I am writing this, I am preparing to lead a mastermind group, oversee the creation of a new training program involving 20 other leaders, and take part in an online TV series of leaders and entrepreneurs. If you were to ask 4th grade Vicki if this was possible, she would have said "NO WAY! I am way too shy to do anything like that."

I was my own glass ceiling back then. Thankfully through the process of AMP, I shattered that ceiling. Despite being introverted, the sky is the limit for this introverted leader.

It can be for you too! Are you ready to AMP up your leadership and go higher? Take that first step and then take the next and the next! Soon you, too, will be seen as a leader and achieve things you never believed possible.

Remember, the world may be noisy and extroverts may seem to be the logical leaders, but introverts make equally fantastic leaders.

AUTHOR VICKI IBAUGH

Vicki Ibaugh is a multi-talented coach and instructional designer with over 20 years of experience creating online courses for Fortune 500 companies, hospitals and government agencies. She now uses her skills and knowledge to show busy entrepreneurs how to experience true freedom by creating courses and programs that allow them to have MORE—time, money and impact. In addition, she is an Amazon best-selling author, certified speaker, chapter leader of the Orlando Chapter of Women's Prosperity Network, certified health coach and a licensed nurse practitioner.

She loves to learn, run, hike, read, and travel. When she is not living in Orlando, she spends time in her happy place of Lake Tahoe with her husband and son. One of her favorite adventures was getting to dive the Great Barrier Reef in Australia.

Vicki's favorite commodity is time, and she is committed to sharing the secret of how to have more time with entrepreneurs who are all too often stressed and bogged down by trading time for dollars. The Course Creation Studio shows entrepreneurs how to leverage their time and their knowledge by creating courses that can be created once and then sold over and over again.

Connect with the Author. . .

Vicki Ibaugh, The Course Creation Coach
Owner of Instructional Assets and The Course Creation Studio
Orlando, FL / Incline Village, NV

Website: www.TheCourseCreationStudio.com (feel free to visit for a free resource tool on course creation)
Social Media:
Facebook: https://www.facebook.com/InstructionalAssets/
Email: Vicki@TheCourseCreationStudio.com

"I failed a million times while chasing success. Leadership is becoming enchanted after the Darkness." ~ Cheryl Jacobs

A Fairytale Story of Enchantment

LEADERSHIP THROUGH THE DARKNESS

CHERYL JACOBS

I never considered myself a leader until I wrote my first book Escape the Darkness into the Enchanted. Writing stirred something inside of me: I saw how I lead from my own experience, how my strength comes from being in deep poverty and emerging to start my own businesses.

Today I have the dream job everyone wants: I get to dress up like a queen or a princess to entertain at birthday parties for young children. I started my company on a hope and a dream after a life of tragedy and recoil.

As a teenager, I became pregnant. Like so many girls my age who paused their life dreams due to pregnancy, I didn't have a clue what I was doing. I had ambitions and dreams in high-school, and ironically, was the last in my class to have a boyfriend. Obviously, the boyfriend ended up being the father of my two children.

I gave up custody of the children to their father after fighting a losing battle. I regret my decision, but know that I cannot go backward and change things, nor can I fix the damage. All I can do today, is to keep moving forward and live the best possible version of myself.

I want to talk to young girls and mothers of young girls for a moment. Ladies, lead your own life based on what you feel is best for you, not what others say is best for you. My life choices led me from one rock-bottom to the next and most of those bad decisions revolved around relationships.

At times, I have had large quantities of money coming in, because one of my choices in career was to dance at bars. I made a ton of money dancing. That set of gigs led me to modeling and then acting. Were these successes due to any ability on my part to lead? No. Men see me as beautiful and sexy, which while true is not the whole truth. For much of my life, I had a secret: I am a smart woman who hides her intelligence.

Coming into my own, and by that, I mean finding something I could fall in love with, took years of heartache and tears. It's my mission to help you avoid those pitfalls for yourself or your daughters.

Let me tell you about my relationship choices.

My first marriage became quickly abusive.

The one shining light from that time was going to aeronautic school. I learned how to fly. Years later I got my license and now am a private pilot—which I totally love. I never gave myself credit for being intelligent because I could effectively use my beauty and looks to make money.

We lived in a filthy apartment. I could not be the mother I wanted to be. I was raised a Catholic and told it is a sin to have babies outside of wedlock. Does this one sound familiar? Because of this old belief, I married the man who fathered my children. We separated when my first child was young, got back together, and then we had a daughter.

His drunken drug parties were just too much. A few years went by and we divorced.

Determined to make something of my life, I allowed him to take custody of the children because I was in no shape to fight. I was beaten down by the system and the agony of feeling like I was unfit to raise my kids.

Between then and now, I have been in two relationships. The most recent mistake (I prefer to consider these relationship disasters as lessons) was getting involved with a narcissist.

Do you know what that word means? It's someone who is so into themselves that that use and mentally abuse women.

A narcissist has a habit of lifting up women, and then emotionally abusing them using isolation and threats of abandonment, and to secretly criticize them in the hidden walls of outside conversation. He did all of this.

This relationship ended because I chose not to stand for his abuse. And, it ended because of Facebook of all things.

Going back a bit, after I divorced my first husband, I jumped head first into every career that paid money to me based on my body, my looks, and my ability to entertain. I sometimes think of this time as riding a roller coaster. It was a time when my life twisted and turned in different directions and around many curves.

One curve led me to modeling where I made more money than I ever thought I could. Well, different money—remember I was a professional dancer at the clubs.

Relationships and business. These two areas are where my ability to lead myself out of the darkness was challenged time and again. Each bad choice led to a different set of self-abuse.

The bar scene and all that went with it was not for me. Letting go of this was hurtful to me, but staying would have been worse. We often will hang on to something painful because it feels normal.

Another curve took me into representing and managing DJ's. That was a fun job that also got to be overwhelming

I Failed a Million Times—At the Success I was Chasing

I was at my wits end when a friend told me about someone she met who performed at kid's birthday parties. A bell went off! I hadn't realized I was searching for a business, but as I researched this idea and did a few parties, I found that I truly love doing this. I developed my business in New York City and now I manage a team of actors who travel all over the North-Eastern US and Midwest doing parties for children.

My most popular character today is Elsa from the movie Frozen. You can see my characters on my Facebook page and my website. I have put so much time and effort into taking control of my life, my relationships, and my business. I hope that you will be inspired.

I am not hiding my intelligence anymore. I have learned hundreds of lessons in my life thus far and look forward to those yet to be experienced. There are three lessons out of the hundreds that I would count as most worth sharing:

Never let anyone tell you that you are not good enough to do what you want to do in life.

Follow your dreams until your life feels better, and you feel empowered.

Reconcile with your inner-self as many time as you need to find your balance.

AUTHOR CHERYL JACOBS

Born & raised near Cleveland, Ohio. I got married at 18, had two beautiful children and divorced at 21. During my divorce, I lived in poverty so poor I had to go to the local church for milk and cheese to feed my two babies. Shortly after, my mother passed of breast cancer at the young age of 43, and my grandmother passed three months later. It was the darkest time of my life.

My life was forever changed. The words of my Mother saying, "Never depend on anyone and always have the capability to stand on your own two feet," was the driving force behind me.

Slowly but surely, I began to heal from all the tragedy in my life. Soon I graduated from Kent State University in aeronautical engineering with honors and started my first business, a modeling and talent agency. I then landed a huge modeling contract with Playboy Book of Lingerie. No nudity!!! This changed my life once again.

My modeling and acting career really took off. I moved to LA and NY to pursue it full swing. I bought my first home and a fishing charter boat and started my second business.

I landed roles on *Law & Order* and the *Sopranos*. My resume consists of over 36 TV and film appearances as well as several print jobs like Romance book covers, catalogs, and runway work.

These days I'm working my eighth business, branding my company KidsPartyCharacters.com, and taking it nationwide to, hopefully, International. Plus, since 2005, I'm a pilot working with the owners of Netjets. Yes, I can teach you to fly a plane.

I've recently published my first book called *Escape from the Darkness into the Enchanted*. My goal is to help people to see that, no matter what life throws at you, it can be overcome with hard work and drive.

Connect with the Author. . .

Website: www.CherylJacobs.org
Social Media
 Facebook: cherylelizabethjacobs
 Instagram: cherylejacobs
 LinkedIn: cheryl-jacobs
 Twitter: @chezr1sque

CHAPTER 22

"True Leaders don't create followers; they create more leaders."

~ *Brenda Dempsey*

She Who Leads

A FEMININE DESIGNED LEADERSHIP FOR TODAY AND BEYOND

BRENDA DEMPSEY

ho is your conscious leader? When someone asks, "Who is a great leader?" Who is the first person who instantly comes to your mind?

Hands up!

Who said, Nelson Mandela or Richard Branson or Barack Obama? Be honest!

Now ask yourself another question, "Why was a man the first person you thought about?"

All your life, you are unconsciously influenced by culture, education, and media with subliminal messages which promote male superiority over female inferiority.

Even if you don't mentally agree, your subconscious mind is suggesting otherwise.

The role of the feminine in Leadership.

Ask yourself this question, "Who are the great female leaders of the last century?"

Did you find it much easier to consider some of the great female leaders? Perhaps one of these: Margaret Thatcher, British Prime Minister (1979-1990); Aviator Amelia Earhart, first woman to fly across the Atlantic alone (1932); Business Woman and Fashion icon Coco Chanel; Ground breaking Scientist Marie Curie or Emmeline Pankhurst, British Suffragette spearheading and changing the voting rights of women. I am sure you have your favorites.

Commonalities of Female Leaders

Consider what these women have in common. Without exception, they each found a cause greater than themselves. This meant that they fought for what they believed in, almost certainly going against the tide of the day, no more so than the role women played in the early part of the twentieth century. Moreover, being highly influential they attracted many followers and supporters who helped them achieve their vision. Their conviction, determination, and perseverance against all odds drove them to achieve great heights, changing the lives of people at the time as well as leaving a legacy for us today.

You could argue they were single minded, forthright and stubborn. In fact, they were visionaries, exceptionally brave, and demonstrated the strength and power of being a woman in a world that was dominated by men. Without a shadow of a doubt they were the pioneers of female leadership. They opened doors for a new breed of women as we stepped into the twenty first century where technology, science and innovation swept our world at a fast and furious pace.

Breaking through the glass ceiling with Purpose

Transitioning from one way of life to another brings resistance, raises fears, and creates uncertainty in many people's minds.

So how do the leading women who stride out in front break through the glass ceiling and embrace the future with excitement, adventure, and a sense of achievement—even before they have climbed their mountain and staked their flag on the peak?

A Leading Lady

Oprah Winfrey is one of today's great leaders whose influence has spanned both the twentieth and twenty first centuries. She epitomizes the qualities that forge the way for female leaders today.

Having a great love of people is one trait that great leaders possess. This heart centered approach promotes each person having their own voice which is valued for its opinions, thoughts, and suggestions. I call this respect.

Connection with your inner self is paramount to stand out from the ordinary. Great leaders like Oprah, know that they do not necessarily have all the answers; it's prudent to know when to seek solutions and ideas from other sources. This makes them extraordinary!

Like all great leaders, Oprah has a vision to be a teacher known for inspiring students to be more than they thought they could be. Listening to the voice within her also created a path for others to follow and seek to find answers that were not in any books; answers that inspired to venture into a new way of thinking. Meditation, the Law of Attraction, and controlling your thoughts and mind are relatively new powers that would create the vehicle for more and more women to raise their voices and take a lead first and foremost in their lives.

Inevitable Change

Women desire to lead their lives in an empowered way rather than subservient. Consider Malala, a young Afghanistan girl, shot by the Taliban as she stood up for the rights of girls in Asian countries to be educated. And Sheryl Sandberg, COO of Facebook who pioneered the *Lean In* movement and is outspoken about the inequality of women.

And Emma Watson who launched the #HeforShe movement because both women and men have a role in the fight against inequality.

What do these famous, courageous, and inspirational women have in common that spans both the twentieth and twenty first centuries? They desire change.

Fusion of Technological Advancement and Human Behavior

The world moves at an incredibly fast pace. Technology waits for no-one and the lightning speed of its development leaves people confused and bemused. One can soon become a technophobe! What has this to do with leadership? She who leads must embrace technological advancement and know how to use this to her advantage.

Unfortunately, the human mind, behaviors, and acceptance of change all move at a slower pace than does technology. There is resistance to change because we like to stay in our comfort bubble (even when we complain about it) and reduce the amount of risk we take. We sabotage our progress by the limits we and society place upon us.

With courage, creativity, and determination, women are first to embrace change. Alignment of both male and female energy begins to create a holistic approach to thinking, feeling, and being. It informs communication, behavior, and actions.

Harmonizing Divine Feminine and Masculine Energy

The rise of the feminine energy in today's world is not fear based. It seeks balance and harmony with the world's masculine energy so that life is led from our heart space and not head space. The Divine Feminine energy is an intelligent energy that contains the quality of intuition, compassion, emotion, creativity, empathy, collaboration, spirituality, holistic thought, and right brain thinking. The qualities of the Divine Feminine energy give us the ability to love and understand one another in a spiritual and holistic way.

The Divine Masculine energy is an intelligent energy that possesses the quality of analytic and rational thinking, competition, determination, linear thinking, logical thought, action, and left brain thinking. It relies too much on math and science to understand life and lack spiritual awareness and creativity.

It is very important to know that the Divine Feminine energy doesn't necessarily represent the female human body and the Divine Masculine energy doesn't necessarily represent the male human body. Each human possesses both feminine and masculine energy and its learning how to control these so we can function in flow to optimize our happiness and success.

A fundamental key to change is 'different action'. As we transitioned from the twentieth century into the twenty first century, there were leaders who continued to control the masses with a very much left-hand side of the brain approach. Behind this there had already been a shift in energy since 2012 and this new Divine Feminine energy has been rising since then. When those who prefer to keep people in their place learn about this new way of thinking they conjure up ways of halting its progress.

A lesson in Metaphor

Like the story of the well illustrates; as the water trickles and you continue to pump, the water soon picks up speed until it is flowing easily from the spout.

This is exactly what has been occurring in the world in terms of leadership with a shift from heavily driven masculine energy to the more creative, heart led feminine energy. In other words, leaders are beginning to realize that the 'boss' mentality of leading does not endure productivity or give value to the rest of the people they are leading. Whereas adopting a more heart led approach where collaboration, team work, and value are implemented to increase motivation, empowerment, and success in attaining outcomes and goals which in turn improves results and progress.

A shifting paradigm from failure to learning

You have probably heard the cliché, *I've learned from my mistakes; I think I'll make a few more*. The adoption of a heart led approach to leadership encourages risk taking because failure is part of the learning cycle and is embraced.

Failure itself lessens the fear of failure.

This progressive way of thinking is being adopted by many of the world's leading companies; Google, Gore, and UK based Nixon McInnes (social media company) who have coined the concept 'Church of Fail' and celebrate mistakes regularly and in a public manner.

This enlightened way of thinking embraces the feminine energy and illustrates beautifully the shift in moving from the masculine head space leading to a more heart based leading. This no blame culture is what makes these companies stand out in leading the way through risk-taking, innovation, and transformation. Awareness of their leadership characteristics, traits, and styles can open doors for more people to mirror this level of success.

Knowing your Leadership Style is Power

There is a Leadership Revolution taking place in the US and across the world. Companies and individuals are no longer impressed with outdated leadership styles and instead are ready to embrace more modern approaches which includes the rise of feminine energy, more heart centeredness, and a more cohesive and collaborative approach to achievement and progress.

Goleman suggests there are six styles of leadership: Commanding, Visionary, Affiliative, Democratic, Pacesetting and Coaching. He sets out to describe them as traits, communication, links to Emotional Intelligence, situations where they work best, and their overall impact on climate. Like most things, adopting leadership styles that strive for balance and harmony creates more efficiency and effectiveness in their implementation.

A Secret to Effective Leadership

A secret to effective leadership is this. Find your voice. Embrace your Truth. Know both your strengths and weaknesses well and then recruit other leaders who are different from you to fill the gaps; listen to them deeply; and trust them completely. Most importantly become aware of your style and know its impact in your leadership. The end result? Better decisions that result in better business.

Modern Styles of Leadership in a changing world include:

Charismatic Leaders focus on personality and charm and are sensitive to member's needs. They exude high-self-belief. They are bold in their risk taking and display unconventional behavior.

Transformational Leadership is one of the most popular styles of leadership today and focuses on effecting revolutionary change through commitment and sharing of vision. Transformational leaders apply passion and energy to their work and inject the same in others.

Visionary Leaders focus on turning dreams into goals and instilling commitment in others through inspiration. They back up their dreams with action. They adopt a partnership approach, look for solutions, and desire a win\win situation.

Transactional Leadership focuses on getting the job done and believes in rewards and punishment. This style of Leadership is the closest to traditional styles of leadership. The subordinates get a salary and other benefits whilst the business has total authority over them.

Servant Leaders focus on the leader as the servant first and leader second. They empower the subordinate and act proactively to inspire them to perform. They demonstrate how more can be achieved together than as an individual.

Agile Leadership is underpinned by Agile Learning which focuses on mastery and expertise in self-awareness to include mental, people, change, and results agility. Agile Leaders who spring to mind are Richard Branson, Maya Angelou, and Mary Kay Ash; they have humility, adaptability, vision and engagement.

Thought Leaders exhibit an advanced leadership style whereby individuals are informed opinion leaders and the go-to experts. They move and inspire people with innovative ideas; turn ideas into reality and know and show how to replicate their success.

Leadership is evolving as is the rise of Divine Feminine Energy. This energy is rising to fuse with the Divine Masculine Energy so it can balance and harmonize human energy, enabling you to live an aligned, happy, and prosperous life. To this end I want to introduce you to a new wave thinking form of leadership–Holistic Leadership.

Holistic Leadership promotes in both genders the balance and harmony in the alignment of divine feminine and masculine energies. This is important to create the flow between each form of energy so you can increase your awareness of each and then adjust your approach to ensure alignment is maintained as much as possible.

A Leading Path

Holistic development is applicable to all aspects of human progress; as individuals, as a team, and as an organization or community. It is the optimum approach in enabling a person or group to achieve their potential without imposing limits. It's having an awareness that we are made up of sum parts and that each part must be nourished and developed, so that the whole is balanced and in harmony to reach its highest potential and beyond.

I believe it's time for a new approach to Leadership on all levels: individual, team, corporation, community, and global. The rise of the Divine Feminine Energy through women who are innate nurturers, have creative flair, and a heart that understands the holistic approach is needed to advance change in our world. Consequently, it is time for women and men to rise to this challenge.

Elements of Holistic Development

It takes courage, resilience, and determination to face change; the greatest change beginning with self. This journey begins with the foundation of Holistic Development and Learning which focuses on the five key elements of Heart, Mind, Soul, Values and Service

A Paradigm Shift

When you consider the evolution of leadership spanning two centuries, the shifting and increasing inclusion of women in prominent positions makes it evident that something is changing. I suggest that this transforming paradigm shift is attributed to the growing awareness and rise of feminine energy within each of us thanks primarily to such platforms as social media, conferences, and the upsurge in personal development.

Notwithstanding theory, it is through my practice of Leadership and my experiences that I have conceived this dynamic Holistic Leadership concept with a synergetic approach which includes contemporary Transformational, Agile, and Thought Leadership underpinned by values, alignment of Divine and Feminine Energies, and service for the greater good.

With over 15 years of leadership experience within education, national social enterprise and most recently a global writing project to bring women and men together through raising the awareness and development of Divine Feminine Energy through stories that focus on 'Pivotal Moments' in life.

Whilst many perceive Leadership as a serious concept, it is vital to have a relaxed, fun, and high vibe energy infused throughout so that you can enjoy every step of the journey including the wins, losses, and challenges that show up along the way. I leave you with the words of Aimee Mullins, Inspirational Speaker, "Come dance with me!"

AUTHOR BRENDA DEMPSEY

Brenda Dempsey (Domestic Abuse survivor, Catalyst and Problem Solver) is a Teacher, Master Coach, Speaker and Author already published in the Anthology Book of Inspiration for Women by Women and soon her own work A-Z of Diamond Success.

She has found a love of writing and uses this to assist other women to raise their voices with their own stories. She is the creator of Pivotal Moments 101—An Anthology Trilogy full of transformational stories of Strength, Courage and Changing Inspiring Hope in others written by women around the globe.

As a Transformational Coach, Brenda successfully empowers, inspires, and uplifts women so they too can be free to live life on their terms and achieve their dreams. Her vision is to create leaders through education and embracing the Diamond ripple effect of Holistic Leadership.

Brenda has founded a charity for Homeless women, focusing in their sanitary and hygiene, called Helping Handbags Worldwide. She is a mother of 4 smart kids and Grandmother to 7 beautiful grandchildren. Brenda loves to travel the world leaving her mark on the lives of those she touches. She lives in Surrey, UK and can be found at:

Connect with the Author. . .

Website: https://www.brendadempsey.co.uk

Social Media

Facebook: https://www.facebook.com/BrendaDempseyDiamondSuccess

Instagram: https://www.instagram.com/brendadempsey/

LinkedIn: https://www.linkedin.com/BrendaDempsey

Email: hello@brendadempsey.co.uk

"Leadership is a fluid process, as we are simultaneously and continuously students and leaders. While traveling the path created by mentors, leaders continue to forge new byways for others–allowing vulnerability by sharing that journey. And not only the pretty parts, sprinkled with glitter, but also those that were built on blood, sweat, and tears. Leaders' service helps others become prepared to grasp the luxury of designing their lives well–so they can live their lives...their way." ~ Chondra Raye Rankin

Death Begets an Awakening

CHONDRA RAYE RANKIN

*E*veryone has a story and someone out there needs to hear your story! Sharing it validates you as a vulnerable, real person. Sharing is imperative—not only the pretty parts, sprinkled with glitter, but also those that were built on blood, sweat, and tears.

People have their own perception of who I am. That's my façade, what I want people to see, but that has not always been in alignment with my inner vision, the true me. Does that mean I'm fake? No. But in realization of this incongruity, I've set out on a journey to mold my exterior, others' perception about me, to mesh with my inner view because, you see...*that's* when the magic occurs.

But, I'm getting ahead of myself.

There's no extraordinarily terrible or life-shattering childhood to tell about. I have always been the square peg trying to fit into the round hole. Honestly, there are many things I don't remember from childhood. Childhood amnesia? A possibility. In all reality, the more significant the event, the longer the memory lasts. (Which means, my childhood was boring? Who knows.) Some events were very memorable and others I remember through photographs and stories I've heard 30,000 times.

That said, my childhood was unusual in many ways!

My dad was a pastor, and he and Mom worked tirelessly toward that end although it took nearly all their resources. I am thankful, now, for a strong foundation in faith, but as a child growing up in a small town, there is a certain stigma, a judgement, associated with you as the Preacher's Kid.

With our lives centered around the church, there were always people around. After services, groups would come over for lunch and hang out all afternoon. We didn't have family vacations—instead, my parents would load our midnight blue Blue Bird school bus (retrofitted, so it was categorized as an RV) every summer to drive cross-country from Iowa to Washington state for church camp. Dad was from Washington, so it doubled as a trip to visit my paternal relatives. This bus was filled with as many as 24 passengers, ranging from extended family to friends, for our annual trip out West.

Through a child's eyes, it sometimes felt like a betrayal to see so much of your parents' time spent being involved with and giving to other people's kids. When others have problems, there is a perception that you have none.

Despite my diligent efforts to achieve perfection, inside I ,knew I never measured up. As in Alanis Morissette's song *Perfect*, I felt love was conditional:

We'll love you just the way you are, if you're perfect.

As the summer wound down and music of the cicadas filled the heavy night air, I was extremely apprehensive about my cousins returning home (after all, they had lived with us all summer!) and the camps with the constant people parade coming to an end. My anxiety was also triggered by returning to school with the accompanying stress and expectation around seeing people who had been out of my life all summer long.

A terribly shy child, I was awkward at making small talk with others and often lacked the self-confidence to look others in the eye. That followed me into high school, and was still present in college—and although I was becoming more self-confident, I had a long way to go, baby!

During junior high school, the restroom at lunch time was often full of pubescent girls who had the world all figured out. The haze of perfume and hairspray was thick in the air (after all, this was Big Hair era!). After using the facilities my usual panic set in at being studied by these popular, confident, pretentious girls (whose world was their oyster).

I immediately escaped the concrete prison, only to hear, "That's so gross! She didn't even wash her hands!"

I fled to safety, my cheeks burning with embarrassment. Humiliation was the icing on the cake that day.

It may not seem like a big deal, but the fact that it is burned into my brain tells me otherwise. I'm probably the only person who still remembers this incident, and it is past time to Let. It. Go. It's past time to shift that memory into the neutral zone.

During high school, I attended an out-of-state percussion camp for several summers. This 2-week camp was way out of my comfort zone as I knew no one there upon arrival. Dorms overlooked the volleyball court, which was often occupied while we were not practicing, having lessons, classes, or giving performances. I never played the game, or went down to the court—but watched from the safety of the second-floor balcony window (all the while, terrified I'd be seen). I couldn't bear the thought of mixing with the others and my paralyzed feet supported that sentiment.

Growing up, I was filled with an inexplicable emptiness and despair; emotions that I clearly couldn't deal with and didn't understand. I knew only that no one understood me and couldn't verbalize why I felt the way I felt. As an adult, I've begun to successfully cope with these issues head on, which has brought me to the space I'm currently inhabiting. I feel gratitude for that journey.

I discovered drawing was a creative outlet that allowed my pain to be expressed. I vividly recall one page in my sketchbook. In it, I depicted my room in rich detail via tones of graphite—I was crying, laying on my back on the floor with anguishing *House of Pain* lyrics scrawled across the page.

Square peg. Round hole.

To combat emptiness and confusion, I quickly recognized that food was a comfort. *And. There. Was. Food!* Freezers of the good stuff. My mom made the best homemade cinnamon rolls. At any given time there were plenty of them in the freezer, waiting to be warmed in the microwave then bathed in delicious butter to turn into a sweetly amazing, gooey treat of carb-filled goodness. The problem was, I did not stop at one. Or two. Not even four. (I liked even numbers, you see.) No. I consumed eight in a sitting. Eight! Why not? That is the best number. That is the most comforting number.

Unfortunately, this was not a one-time occurrence. If no cinnamon rolls were available, another carb-ridden food would do. Yes, please! A warm homemade waffle with ice cream melting in its many crevices. A warm molasses cookie (with added butter!)? Are you drooling yet?

I'm not. These days, I don't even crave it as I type these words. Whole foods and the foods that make me feel my best are the foods I crave. Do I weigh 100 pounds? No. Not even close. But upon closing in on these destructive body memories, not only does my self-image improve, but pounds are actually released. Talk to me this time next year and see what I have to say about it!

A natural progression toward leadership in my life took place as I began teaching what I learned. For two decades, I taught piano lessons and continue to teach Bible lessons to all ages. Teaching really makes you learn much more than you ever do as a student and taking on this role has also enabled me to overcome crippling fear and shyness. I've found in recent years that there are an exponential number of people online and in social media who ache to uncover answers. People like myself and like you who covet a better way in life. Creating your own niche and knowing there are creative and *lucrative* ways to make a living online, grows your audience—and more importantly, allows you to serve more people with greater reach than ever before!

Life is Short

A pivotal event impacting my leadership journey occurred in early 2014. One afternoon while working, I received a call from the police, informing me that my older sister was trying to contact me. With my heart like a rock in my stomach, I made the dreaded call. It *had* to be devastating news. She couldn't say it, could not speak aloud the impossibility that occurred.

"It's Dad. I found him...I'm sorry."

I asked. I needed to know. I had to hear the words. The panic in my voice rose to a high pitch, "Is he dead? IS. HE. DEAD?"

She said in a weary tone, "Yes."

The conversation ended abruptly, and surrounded by cubicle walls, I stifled violent sobs, gasping for air and wanting to wake from this nightmare. He was just 64 and had been to the doctor two weeks prior, leaving the office with a clean bill of health. And yet, while up late reading the night before, he had suffered a massive, fatal heart attack.

My younger sister and I were propelled into unexpected leadership roles that summer, taking over for many of the roles Dad would have filled at our State church conference. We've both continued filling in many of these roles, and they have become a more natural fit.

In addition to being a pastor, Dad worked in maintenance at an elementary school. Although he loved the kids and most of the people working there, there were some occurrences that were highly stressful, causing him unhappiness and depression. Forty years he worked at this job. He retired after four decades and was able to spend only two years enjoying retirement before his light was extinguished.

I always wanted to do something epic for my hardworking parents, but never had that chance. Dad's unexpected death taught me harsh life lessons. I knew I must live differently, and although had no idea how to do it, knew there had to be another way! This was something I was compelled to find—and then, fueled by passion to serve—help others achieve their own ambitions!

This evolution has been one of progressive learning. Napoleon Hill had this stuff figured out a century ago!

My mind often screams, *Why is mindset not taught in schools?!*

But it never will be. It is easier to control people who have no fire; people who are okay with the status quo. When you learn the truth, you want to start a revolution to effect positive change!!

Once you awaken, it's hard to go back to sheep.

Once awake, you'll be so excited about every minute of every day that you don't want to waste even a single moment! Vibrational frequency is raised and your purpose is so clear to you that the excitement often keeps you awake at night!!!

Does this mean I must only be positive?

Absolutely not. It is not healthy to ignore part of ourselves. It's all there...the good, the bad, and the ugly! It's necessary to acknowledge and work to understand our Shadow side, so we can choose what affects us—and exercise more control. There will always be light and dark, but it's our choice which has more power!

Throughout life, I allowed insecurities and doubts to hold myself back from success, whether that be in relationships, financially, spiritually, or otherwise. Having been in emotionally and verbally abusive relationships, I celebrate that those chapters are closed–those experiences of betrayal are dead to me now. They have been acknowledged, forgiven and purged from my life. These days, I hold my breath a little less and walk with a little more swagger.

That old personality, the one that cut me off from interacting with people and living my life to its fullest, no longer serves me. I've been diligent in creating a new personality, an abundant, highly engaged personality that sees no barriers to success. Meditation with prayer and feeding my body with proper nutrients are bringing me much closer to the me that I desire. I've become totally alive!

I deserve that.

I have always deserved that.

And so have you.

There is more than enough abundance for us all.

In this new reality being created, if I can affect only one person—*One Person*, then it is all worth it.

Do I think I can change the world? Yes, and I will. With you by my side.

AUTHOR CHONDRA RAYE RANKIN

Chondra R. Rankin is a Musician, Designer, and Online Marketing & Success Coach. Her passion lies in connecting with others at a deep level and helping them gain new perspectives with the end goal being to positively impact their lives! She has been an ongoing contributing author to her church's state newsletter and regularly shares insights in her blog.

> *"The best way to predict the future is create it."*

Whether you attribute the above quote to Peter Drucker or Abraham Lincoln, there is no doubt it's a powerful statement.

This especially resonates in the female community as there has been a movement toward empowerment in the last several decades to level the gender playing field. To realize we can create this aids women in discovering and wielding the tools to produce that desired future.

Born and raised in Iowa, Chondra appreciates the simple life of rural areas and small towns but loves traveling extensively, learning much from the many countries she has been blessed to visit. The true connection in life is celebrating both our similarities and our differences!

Helen Keller said it best, "Life is either a daring adventure or nothing at all!"

Chondra shares details about her life that have never been shared before in this chapter. The writing left her feeling vulnerable—but she knows that it is vital to share her story with others; to show them they are not alone in their struggles and circumstances. She encourages everyone reading this to share their story. Someone out there needs to read it!

Connect with the Author. . .

Website: www.ChondraRankin.com
Social Media
Facebook: https://www.facebook.com/chondra.rankin
Facebook: https://www.facebook.com/ChondraCoaching/
Twitter: https://www.twitter.com/chon_ran
Instagram: https://www.instagram.com/chondrarankin

"Stand in your Truth and Commit with Confidence to a High Standard." ~ Judith Lynne Miller-McKay

Say YES! More Often Than You Say No!

JUDITH LYNNE MILLER-MCKAY

*D*id I have a rigid black-and-white plan for my life when I was a young girl? I remember an emphatic, *No!* I also remember I loved to travel and still do. That began at an early age with our summer vacations when our family of six would pile in the station wagon and travel to Georgia and Florida to visit relatives and play in the Gulf of Mexico. What I liked best was making new discoveries. Each summer we did the same thing, only traveling to the Upper Peninsula of Michigan where we camped, hiked, played, fished, and swam in the cold Michigan lakes. It was always a new and curious adventure of fun and discovery.

My parents liked to take the road less traveled, going around the next bend to see what we could discover. I think I inherited my travel bug. It also showed up in my grandmother who traveled out West after farming season was over and would always return to share photos and stories and say, "Someday, you must go West, young lady."

I was fortunate to be given the opportunity to take part in high school junior and senior trips to Washington D. C. and New York City.

I think that leadership was evident in me even then because the first trip I took was in my junior-year and the other was as a senior asked to be an assistant to the teachers for the next junior high school trip.

I still remember the impact made on my young and receptive mind and heart seeing those big cities and the possibilities. I was in heaven. The world was opening up to me–I learned there was more than living in my community in southern Ohio. Mind you, I loved all things about my Ohio–that was where I began; my foundation is there. Spending time in Michigan, Florida, and Georgia were also happy memories of fun and discovery.

After high school, my dreaming turned to finding a job traveling. The reality of being a young woman fresh out of high school and wanting to earn money from her first job (not a travel job) threatened to overwhelm my enthusiasm for work, so my sister and I decided to take a vacation. We knew we wanted to do a sun and fun beachy vacation, but didn't know where. A lady travel agent, introduced by a friend, had just returned from some exotic place in the world to scope out new vacation destinations for her customers. She became our travel planner and sent us to Cozumel before it got on the map. And so we did, and it did.

Then and there I decided that is what I wanted to do–travel around the world, get paid for it, provide a service and make decisions, while fulfilling my dreams. I could even take people on tours around the world. I had never taken classes to become a travel agent; I just knew I had that passion for curiosity through travel and discovery. I convinced this lady travel agent to meet with the male partners of the family-owned business for which she worked. During our meeting, I convinced them to give me OJT (on-the-job-training). When they said yes, I was on cloud nine.

I lived in the same city where I grew up, had my own apartment and had a job that was okay. I am the eldest of four siblings. I respected my parents and was still certain that they knew what was best for their young daughter. I remember my mother and dad saying many times that I should be able to take care of myself and not be dependent on anyone financially. They each had their own version of this. Mother wanted me to not have to rely on anyone and to be self-sufficient, wanting the best and to enjoy my life. Dad would say how important it is to get a good job, to save at least ten percent of my salary every paycheck, and not to spend frivolously. He did not emphasize being happy. I like to think he did want that for me. They both said to always have good work ethics and values, work hard and do a good job for your employer, be honest and kind and don't get caught up in company gossip, and have confidence. That guidance has taken me well through my professional career and my life.

I came home and told my parents about this job offer and how happy I was. Dad looked at me and said, "You don't want to do that. Get a real job and save your money and then you can travel." And so I did. He knew best. Or so I believed at the time.

No Regrets

I have talked to people over the years about this—from spiritual leaders to wise men and women—for their thoughts. Finally, I heard I what I needed to hear to settle my heart and soul and move on. Forgive and know that he wanted the best for you so that you could have the best for you. Parents living in the depression and old-world school heritage had their own beliefs to live by. Feelings, at least from my dad, were not important when it came to work. I struggled with this for years and finally found peace with it by listening and learning about me and what kind of life I wanted.

Over the years, I worked for many companies because that was my choice. I was single and curious to see what made companies tick—what was their structure, their mission, their ethics. I knew I did not want to stay with a company for the proverbial gold watch. That gives me the shudders now to even think about that. I enjoyed learning about types of businesses and who ran the ship—who were the women leaders, and their story.

One day out of the clear blue I received a phone call from the company's personnel office that they had received a wire from a company offering me a position as Financial Manager/Budget Analyst in England. There was no question—I knew I wanted to do this, and so I did with excitement and support from family and friends. Off into the wild blue yonder I went with enthusiasm and not knowing a soul. I was foot-loose, single and fancy-free, and the world was at my fingertips. What more could a girl ask? I jumped in head first with no expectations and had the time of my life, well, almost...there was the job to do. I had to keep reminding myself if it wasn't for the job, I wouldn't have these opportunities to travel, explore, and meet people in that part of the world.

I learned about leadership in this role. Working together with British and American employees presented new challenges. Each had their own value sets, their preferred way things were to be done, and what they expected from me as a manager. There is power in being the boss. And it was a rush when they came to me with questions and I had answers. Most of the time it was not do as I say, but working in teams and one-on-one discussion. There were plenty of British and American men and women who I networked with, but there was no mentor, no real guidance or support group. I had to draw on everything I knew and be open to learning more. There were many lessons learned, some easy and some challenging. But we did what we needed to do with trust, and openness, and communication.

Two-and-a-half years later, I married an American who had lived in England for fifteen years. We moved to the Silicon Valley, and I continued being a financial manager/budget analyst. Who would have ever guessed? Marriage was the last thing on my mind. I was having the time of my life discovering this new-to-me Old World. And now a new and exciting adventure began.

I continued working as a financial manager in various states and continued in this role when we went to Japan where a new world of culture and traditions opened to me. Going in with no expectations and open to the possibilities and opportunities, I met people and did things I could have never ever imagined; one example was teaching English to Japanese company employees. That was another challenge using my leadership skills while learning the nuances of the Japanese culture. I thoroughly enjoyed this exercise, and I felt a connection. I have friends who stay in touch. I and another lady fulfilled a shared dream by planning a trip to China. We also took advantages of opportunities to travel throughout the Far East. I was working in countries and traveling to places I would have never guessed.

I worked as a Financial Manager/Budget Analyst again, this time with Americans and Japanese. As in England, different mindsets about work ethics and values and management styles showed up. There were many challenges and many learning curves. Being a budget analyst worked for me—it was more of a grey area to be creative with. I got into that. And it was another important tool for decision-making.

Six years later, way too short, it was time to give someone else an opportunity to live in and experience that ancient land. It was a bittersweet day when I left Japan. That's another story. I have returned once and hope to visit again.

Work Ethics and Mindset

Leadership always has challenges. Mine showed up working in three entirely different cultures, American, English and Japanese. These jobs served me well financially, but I realized that in the long run this was not my cup of tea. Spiritually and creatively, there was a void. Thank goodness, I was of strong resolve and did my best, drawing on many of those wise words of wisdom over the years.

After a while, I made an important decision. I knew it was time to leave my career as a financial manager. Being an accountant in management took me many places and challenged me beyond limits, most of which I enjoyed. New discoveries—new people, new places, learning more about me. I was traveling and getting paid for it while living in different states and countries. Who would have ever guessed?

My parents would have been happy. I was too, and especially as I now receive a pension. Maybe I can say that I even did it my way, with the encouragement and support of others.

Glass ceilings never entered my mind that that was somewhere I must strive to attain. I trusted my instincts. I could do and did whatever I wanted. It wasn't always perfect, but overall the work I did served me well and vice versa; I was happy. I still feel that way today. I still live by my motto–Communicate, Listen, Trust, Be Open, and Flexible, and you never know the opportunities that abound.

Montana–Next Place to Plant Seeds.

One of the opportunities that presented itself and I said YES to, was at the public radio station in our new community. Even though I am comfortable with public speaking, usually in leadership roles, and doing TV commercials, I had never done radio. The radio beckoned. It spoke to my curiosity. A new discovery! What did I know? What began as a *Yes* turned into two-and one-half years of a one-hour weekly talk show that I produced and hosted.

It opened another insight of who I am and what excited me and still does. Curiosity in meeting people, learning and having the opportunity to share people's stories with others that they might have an ah-ha moment, food for thought, events–something to learn, to get excited about, to dream about–I was finding my calling. These principles carry me into my current radio show.

When we moved to Washington, I said a sad goodbye to my Montana public radio show. I kept reaching out and exploring–that curiosity thing. I took acting lessons and played on a different stage. I wrote a play, directed it and it was performed in the theater. This was yet another chance to get to know me better and understand how I resonate in the world. I thrived by being true to myself and acknowledging my gifts, not shying away any more.

Lead her ship–I have been doing that and have never been happier than when I am producing and hosting my radio show in Colorado

Springs for the same reasons I had when hosting my first radio show. I continually make decisions and network while being my own boss. This ship could not be run alone. Nor would I want to run it alone; it is still takes a team. Sometimes and many times, I know there are people I can reach out to for wise food-for-thought discussions, and vice versa. Amazing things can happen when you listen while following your heart and instincts. Leadership roles can show up in a variety of ways and take you many places. Be open.

As I look back on my career, would I have done things differently? It's easy to second guess, and that takes time and energy I don't care to expend. I do know I learned a lot about people, leadership, management styles, expectations, trust, communication, team playing, and me. I know I did the best I could and I am grateful for the opportunities that came along AND that I said YES. I also know I never ever would have imagined the places (not just countries) that this journey has taken me.

Here are some thoughts that I have garnered over the years:

- Be strong in your convictions and listen to your feelings and instincts. They can be powerful.
- Communication is imperative, including good, clear listening.
- Do your homework before saying yes or no and never be afraid to ask questions.
- Don't compromise your principles. And have the guts and courage to do the right thing and know what that looks like.
- Walk the talk.

When talking with other women in leadership, I hear a similar message. Communication, listening, trust, honesty, kindness, strength of character, and being supportive in team playing while doing your best profits you, the team, and the company. Never be afraid to be a mentor. We all need those wise words from others. After all is said and done, we are all connected.

Be open and flexible as much as possible to opportunities. Say *Yes* more than you say *No* because you never know where and how that opportunity can take you. I trusted my instincts and didn't second guess them. I knew what felt right and went with it into the unknown with eyes wide open. Little did I know! (Probably more than I thought I knew). That is how I have lived my life so far. I didn't know the outcome but knew it was the right thing to do. I speak to this about my professional and personal life.

Life has many lessons. Be Curious! Be Passionate, be confident and trust you. You can be pleasantly surprised while making a difference. Enjoy the Journey. Have fun and take care.

I continue to travel, though I must say, I now travel by choice not connected with a travel agency, since I have been there, done that.

The journey continues. YES!

AUTHOR JUDITH LYNNE MILLER-MCKAY

Judith is a consummate traveler believing that traveling is one of the best educations in the world. She is also professional photographer, playwright and author, participating in a published Anthology by AAUW women, Intersecting Voices, Women who Write Beneath the Peak. She is an Ohio gal now living in Colorado Springs by way of circumventing the world and having a bunch of curiosity.

A financial manager in her past life, a degree from the University of Maryland, and being a lifelong student and teacher has taken her on a wild and wonderful ride.

She continues her sense of connecting through her radio show and podcast, Voices and Views, to offer people and organizations an opportunity to share their stories of how they show up and support way beyond local community. Showing up with faith, trust, and gratitude, as well as having friends and fun always adds up to a rich adventure.

Connect with the Author. . .

Social Media
Facebook: https://www.facebook.com/voicesandviews.KCMJ/
Email: jlmmckaycos@gmail.com

"If your actions inspire others to dream more, learn more, do more, and become more, you are a leader." ~ *John Quincy Adams*

Leadership through Law of Attraction in Action

RACHELE MILLIONS

W hen asked to write about leadership from the single mother point of view, I honestly thought I would not be able to do it. My life was at a crossroads when I got divorced from my son's father. So many thoughts of failure and shame entered my mind. Today I am the mother of a 20-year-old son who makes me very proud. I am also proud to be a Christian and love the Lord, trusting him to navigate my whole path, including the path of a leader within my own home and career.

My leadership journey includes that I am part of a Network Marketing Company. Many people shy away from talking about their Network Marketing business, but I want to say that it is my business that keeps me afloat, and allows me to continue on a path developing leadership skills that help me stay a good role model for my son.

Being a mother of a young adult son has its own bumps and bends, but it's always rewarding. The choice I made to delve into network marketing has helped me be a better mother and leader. By practicing shifting my mind from pain to power, I was able to bridge the gap in my own mind between perceived failure and proud success.

How does the above story tie into my journey to leadership through the Law of Attraction? It simply was the path I chose as I was pulling myself up. I have learned many skills for moving energy after emotional trauma, and the Law of Attraction was the first modality I attempted during the hardest transition of my life.

When I decided to write this chapter, I knew it would include an opportunity for you to learn real skills through reading my story. That's why I chose to share the five most valuable leadership lessons found within the Law of Attraction philosophy. Before we jump into the lessons, I want to share the basic Law of Attraction process.

The Law of Attraction works through a combination of emotions and beliefs. When you make a decision to work with this type of thinking and living, you will encounter deep resistance within yourself. The resistance is there to tell you that you are about to 100 percent change some part of your life. For example, let's say you have no money. Like the thousands of people just like you, you are well aware of the reality that you have no money in your bank; you have no signs of money anywhere. From this starting point, you decide you want to find a new way; you want to shift your life's paradigm and the Law of Attraction comes to your mind.

When you embrace the Law of Attraction, the first thing you will be asked to do is to shift your beliefs around money. I am sure you have heard this before, many times. Well, my theory is that you cannot shift what you are not yet aware of. You must learn to be aware of what your beliefs are at any moment. For example, saying, "I love money and money loves me," may feel fraudulent or plain wrong because your eyes see no money. This is where you have to cultivate a belief in the unseen.

This example is meant to illustrate what can show up for you once you decided to attract what you want. Rather than lament about what you don't have, the attraction method asks you to believe you have that which you do not see. You will combine new words with new energy and start a massive shift in your life.

Leadership through attraction is a skill you will always need. Leading the way for others to believe in more than they currently have helps them also be better leaders.

Five Leadership Lessons

Each lesson is designed to shift your frame of mind from poverty to a prosperous existence. Take a moment and get out some paper. These lessons are interactive and you'll want to take time to think about and respond to each.

1. *Forget Everything You Know*

Lesson one shows you why there may be low spots in your life and how to create better choices and better paths. You were born with a set of beliefs that attach to your childhood, that grow up with you as an adult, and will remain with you—unless you shift them.

For your first lesson, write down ten things you believe about money and be very raw and honest.

Go back into your memories of money and see what shows up for you. You will want to make notes about the emotions that show up for you.

2. *Decide what You Want to Experience*

Now that you have gone back into your memory for just a bit and you have felt the emotions that surround the topic, it's time to decide what you want to experience.

Rather than make a list of what you want to receive, you will make a list of what you want to experience. Being a leader requires you to analyze and assess how you lead. By deciding the experience you want to create, you can help your followers do the same. Examples might be:

- I want to feel the joy and freedom of driving across country for as long as I feel the urge.
- I desire to feel supported and loved by my clients who trust me with their careers.

In the Law of Attraction, adding emotion to your affirmations is a power boost.

3. Act as If

Next, you want to get in the habit of acting As If rather than thinking about What If. In steps one and two, you were asked to locate your old beliefs around money, a topic that surrounds every other topic in attraction living. You were also asked to create a feeling of the experience.

Now you will start your Act as If journal. As you identify the things you desire to attract and the experiences you desire to create, you want to nail this down through writing.

Get a journal that feels good to you, even if it's a heavy duty spiral notebook. Writing is the doorway to receiving.

4. Practice and Learn to Give

Steps one through three teach you how to find the blocks in your beliefs, create your ideal experience, and journey your As If. It's time for practical lessons, real life experiences that happen outside of your house, laptop, and notebook.

Receiving is the doorway for you to prove yourself right. You can think, shift, and be wealthy. It's also a time to learn to give.

This is a fun exercise to do if you are serious about attracting what you want to experience. Go to Starbucks or your favorite store that sells gift cards and pick up a $5 gift card. Go up to the cashier to pay for it and have him or her agree to give the prepaid card to the next person who checks out. In this exercise, you are telling God that you want to receive, and you want to give. You must be able to receive in order to master the art of attracting the ideal experiences you desire.

5. Be Accountable

The final lesson in our 5-part mini-series, is to get on Facebook and do a live video announcing your new vision. Or share with five people who will hold you accountable.

Put yourself in front of people and clarify your intentions. This is powerful and adds fuel to your manifestation fire. You are stuck for one reason or another because you have not moved toward your dream. The more you proclaim your intended results, the more they solidify in your current reality.

Through shifting your inner paradigm out of old beliefs into new beliefs, you set the energetic checkpoint for getting what you need and what you want. Old beliefs are often so far away from who you are at your core that they seem almost foreign when you turn the light of awareness toward them.

God made us all in his image and has instructed us to live as if we were HIM. My life is not perfect, by no sense of the word, but I do feel that I have a strong leadership ethic in work and in life. I would love for you to find me on social media through the links below so I can get to know you better.

Leadership is the ability to first lead your own experience, and second to be a leader for someone else. Attraction marketing in business is using all of your tools to create the flow of paying clients you want to see in your company. Attraction living, in a personal sense is about having the experiences you desire with no guilt or shame.

AUTHOR RACHELE MILLIONS

During the years I was earning my bachelors in Elementary Education with a minor in Political Science and then my Masters in Leadership Development, I never expected that I would use my education and natural-born skills to start my network marketing career in 2003. Since then, I have reached the top rank in two companies. Not bad for a girl born and raised in Oklahoma. Today, when I'm not working at the business I love and helping women to be successful leaders, I enjoy spending time with my son.

Connect with the Author. . .

Website: https://soulsisters.shiftingretail.com/Default.aspx
Social Media
Facebook: https://www.facebook.com/profile.php?id=1042566171

"Leadership is Crafting your Path to the Sunny Side of Life, Learning by Doing, Then in Turn Inspiring, Encouraging, and Empowering Women to Do the Same." ~ *Roxanne Lynch*

A Penny a Nail

LIFE LESSONS ON LEADERSHIP FROM MY FATHER

ROXANNE LYNCH

*P*icking up nails that had fallen from the cabin my daddy built when I was a little girl taught me many lessons in leadership, and in the value of belief. Growing up, I lived in the meadows, creeks and forests. At almost any time you could find me outside, somewhere on the family farm. Surrounded by hundreds of acres of land and livestock, I worked with my family, even as a little one.

One of the greatest childhood memories I had was when my family was living in a big old Army tent on the land while dad was building our cabin. Every time a nail would fall from Dads fingers and roll off from the roof top, my Dad would say, "I will pay a penny a nail."

That was all it took to get my brother, and I excited.

"We are going to be rich," I would say to my brother. Knowing that we could do a little work and get a little money gave us the greatest joy. It became a big game seeking the glint of sun off the head of the nails hidden in the grass.

I tell my clients and team members, that, "It's not what you have, it's what you can do or experience that is important."

See, growing up, we had friends nearby but most of our family lived a day long drive away. We could save up our money and pack up and travel to our uncles and aunts to walk the beaches, collect seashells and driftwood, or fish and swim in the tidal pools, and hike in woodland parks. We loved to work for the creation of memories and life experience. This has been my leadership philosophy in life and in my present work.

We were taught that the experience of earning money and doing something with it like creating memories, travelling, or spending time with family and friends was the reward—and not the money itself. This created a strong foundation within me, that money is a tool to dreams, activities, and memories; just like the hammer was used to lay the tin on the cabin roof. It is what lies within and beyond that counts. That I what I now teach others as part of my own business. We were taught to love working for the experience. To this day, this is my leadership philosophy.

How many pennies do you have and what would you do, if money were never an issue?

Build your Business Like Your Life Depended on It

When you build your business like your life depends on it, then your life can depend on your business. How's that for word magic? Building a business is about networking and relationships, but it's also about making money and enjoying life more. A life well-lived will have ups and downs and challenges. The fun part is looking at challenges as if they are lessons in hiding. Every struggle has opportunity to be discovered and to learn from. Seek the sunshine within. Seek the lesson in every stumble. Challenges and adventures will take us out of our present state of normalcy and provide us with the ability to break the patterns and habits that bind us to our current fate.

Everything that you have done and experienced has brought you to your today. What you do today will bring you to your tomorrow.

You can break the ineffectual patterns and non-productive habits with reflection, re-focused intent, and purpose. New patterns can bring us forward in a positive way within life and business.

Being consciously aware of patterns that pop up as challenges is the first step in being a leader in business. I often say, "Success Loves Speed." Think of how a little snowball can turn into a massive snowball as it gains speed, momentum, and girth rolling down a hill.

In the beginning the little snowball has a challenge. It must gain momentum during the slow part of its roll. We, to face challenges in the early days of working toward a goal. The challenges of the slow part of our journey force us to think and do beyond the easy, routine, and normal. When we think about this from a business aspect, this time can be tough because we expect different results by doing different things.

It's an important thing because this change can help us discover what's on the other side. When we embrace and seek learning through struggle, we transcend normal and get closer to our goals.

When we begin to do different, we receive different. Remembering to pause, reflect, and re-align, we change our thinking, habits, and patterns. We create this new ripple and create new results, positive change. The world seems new, fresh, and exciting!

Remember that our current results in life and business are a reflection of our current actions which is a reflection of our current habits and actions, which in turn stem from our thoughts.

Change your thoughts,

Change your actions and habits,

Change your results.

Yes, you can do this!

My Four C's

A strong plan of action built on a foundation helps create faster movement toward our goals. I love helping inspire women to stand out and shine. There is much goodness out there. It is there for us to have in any aspect of our lives.

Anyone and everyone who is a success, has done things a certain way. Success takes tenacity. Successful people have created a daily map or blueprint which they follow each day. They wake up every day and know what they have to do. Successful ladies check their compass and ensure they are on track with their goals and dreams, taking time to reflect on what is working, what isn't, and adjusting their plan and actions. When successful leaders put their head on the pillow at night, they know what they want to do the next day.

Today I want to share with you what I call my Four Cs—four habits that successful people develop and maintain.

Be Consistent

Being consistent requires that you start small. Do one thing every day and start to do it better. Get up in the mornings and do the same things but better. Being realistic and giving tasks and projects the right amount of time is key to getting to success faster, and to getting different results. You must build a consistency plan. Do those actions long enough so you can have an opinion of how it is working (or not) for you. Create a daily action plan to stretch yourself beyond your comfort zone. No one climbed to the top of a mountain without some pains. You must cultivate *consistency*!

Expand Your Connections

Creating a strong network starts with building connections with people. You must find real friendships, relationships where you can build a team and mastermind. The type of communication within your connections can be online. Reconnect with past friendships and build innovative ways of being consistent with connections. You can find people to meet, locally or online. You can find friends AKA online pen pals all on social media. Find a group that will follow you. Get past being afraid of making new connections. Find friends and connections by asking and listening. You can develop friends and connections in groups that you have a deep passion or interest in. You can choose to learn and teach, empower and inspire.

Offer Engaging Content

What do you share with your tribe? If you are putting engaging information on your social media timeline, you are starting to build great content. You can share your blog, free offer, videos, and more to your walls that will attract others because of the value you give and offer.

Attraction marketing helps you develop your servant heart. Look to use your content to engage people and to encourage people to come to you. It's so much fun when you approach delivering your message with a servant's heart.

Take all the other stuff off your social media and share your valuable content. Do it in a unique way. Do it your way. Be the real authentic you. Be raw and allow yourself to be a bit vulnerable too.

You want to work with those who are wanting and willing. Let go of people you don't click with, you don't have time to chase people.

Serve don't Sell! Seek the connection not the cash! It is a known fact in business, Money follows Value, so become a person of value!

Human Consideration

Allow yourself to learn and stumble and forgive yourself. Seek the lesson in every interaction through reflection. Sometimes people are in their own story. Being considerate in all your connections, providing valued content, is the best way to show that you care and are compassionate.

Add goodness to your heart, mind, and soul. Being considerate is empathy at its finest.

My favorite quote is one I created, *"Lose the mask of perfection to make a deeper connection."*

My father taught me that if you believe in being RICH, then you will attract all the right people, be in the right places at the right times, and attend the right events to experience your belief.

The Camping Trip

Working an online business puts me spending hours in front of the computer. I find that it's a good idea to get out of the house and onto a dirt road experience. My daddy taught me about loving the simple things in life, so recently my husband and I decided to hit the road. We are both very spontaneous people possessing what I call Gypsy Feet.

We went off the grid for some dirt road therapy. The place we decided to camp was about an hour's drive away on a country road. Our campsite was brilliantly faceted. The waters are divided up on top of our Continental Divide here in our Rocky Mountains, it's a place where part of the water will go to the Atlantic and part to the Pacific. On the way, we talked about the last time we each went camping. I was 14 or 15 years old the last time I went camping, like in a tent or in the back of a truck. I'm talking roughing it. The last trip with my dad we forgot our coffee cups, so we had to eat the beans to drink the coffee.

The memories we make when we just do things are an incredible lesson. Sometimes when we wait for perfect, when we are focused on preparing and planning, we never get to experience the amazing beauty of a blessing. Waiting too long can kill your dreams. I believe in practicing spontaneity. We did not plan our camping trip. My husband and I decided to just jump in! We laughed and threw stuff in the car. We just got up and went. We grabbed a cooler and ice. It was fun.

Affirm Your Worth Daily

I have built my newest business from Facebook and have used the tried-and-true method of daily affirmations to build the know, like, and trust factor of my activated tribe.

Here are a few affirmations that I love to share.

- There are no limitations in my life. I give myself full permission to shine as bright as a million suns!
- When you are feeling off course, scattered, unfocused, overwhelmed, detoured, recognize that those feelings are a key, they are a way through that moment. The challenge is to take a deep breath, pick the small detail of what is next, and Do It!
- Find calm in the storm of your mind then think and create action; ever so small, ever so delicate. This is the cure to the feeling or the belief that your life at that moment is going to Hell in a handbasket.
- When you're feeling uneasy, don't let yourself be off course. Ask yourself, "How do I turn it around?" Then take a new path, act, and do!
- Do not think those feelings of being off course, and discouraged as failure, take them as they really are as a nudge in a better truer direction.
- I am Roxanne Lynch and I love supporting women in creating new and exciting paths for their lives.

As a dedicated Network Marketing (MLMer), I proudly rejoice in having a business that my life can depend on, one that gives me boundless joy. Look for me on Facebook Live, encouraging, supporting, and teaching. I would love to connect with you, too.

AUTHOR ROXANNE LYNCH

Roxanne Lynch was born on Vancouver Island British Columbia and as a young girl moved up to rural Cariboo Country near 100 Mile House, BC. Moving to Alberta at 19 to attend college, she now lives in Edson AB with her husband; her grown children and parents living nearby.

Roxanne was 38 when she moved to town. She sold all her Foundation Quarter Horses and bought a Harley Davidson. She loves to spend time in her yard and garden and play in her flower beds. She and her family share big love of travel. Her husband Bob says she is afflicted with what he calls Gypsy Feet. Running a successful online business is a perfect fit for her busy family commitments and their travel loves.

When she was 43, she was first introduced to a Network Marketing (Multi-level Marketing) company and promptly fell flat on her face on social media. She struggled for years, going thousands into debt. Then in the spring of 2015 she was introduced to Attraction Marketing and applied the formula within her business, and her world changed!!

Roxanne is an energetic entrepreneur (affiliate marketer and MLMer) and an inspired compassionate Network Marketing Business Coach. She truly seeks to understand the struggle and is extremely creative helping bring her clients and teammates to what she calls, the Sunny

Side of Life. It is her goal to educate and encourage them to show up on social media with a true servant heart; and thereby to Stand Out and Shine Online.

Roxanne has been interviewed by other Top Earner Teams and readily shares out her best tips and tricks to shorten ladies learning curves. Her secret to success lies in sharing everyday solutions to ease the struggles of online business owners. She has ranked multiple times in her primary business and crossed numerous stages to received awards recognizing personal business achievements. Today she provides personal one-on-one training and education. Her newest online adventure, one that brings much excitement, is to team with global business partners from Kenya and Copenhagen to build her next online social media training course.

Connect with the Author. . .

Social Media
Facebook: https://www.facebook.com/roxanne.lynch.75
Blog: www.roxannelynch.com
Email: roxanne@roxannelynch.com

"Leadership is the ability to see wholeness in the appearance of being broken; to promote choice and compassion in completing the whole."
~ *Rachelle Manieri*

There is No Crying in Bootcamp

RACHELLE MANIERI

*I*t is 2017. The oldest of my four children is 26 years old and the youngest is 17—a senior in high school. Life as a Mom looks different when your last child is in high school. The last three years have been a transformative time for me. It was at the beginning of this, I came to a realization that my children were growing up. Like really. Growing. Up. And I was nervous for them, for me. As I watched them becoming actual, grown, independent people, I to realized that I had developed a leadership role without even knowing it, because they showed me that I had taught them well.

Unfortunately, some of what I was seeing that I taught them was not helpful. In fact, some of what I was seeing mirrored back to me was heartbreaking.

It has been during this transformation time in my life that I have become aware of how our bodies hold trapped trauma and pain; how they speak to us. I learned that I was not a victim, that I could listen to my body, change my story, and release trapped patterns. I learned that I GET to live a whole life; that we ALL get to choose. I learned that I am committed to choice, compassion, and awakening truth.

In the past, I worked with the military in a specific, specialized role. I was a subject matter expert in water survival and the first female hired to work at my command with my division of approximately 45 fleet and special program male service members and civilians.

I was of the mindset that it was my job to work hard and never show pain—anything you can do, I can do too. Maybe not as fast, but I can do it. For me, this was an adventure in dismantling the Glass Ceiling Mindset. Working with that many men created a desire in my soul to become more than I ever imagined. It drove me to a fierce determination to do anything a man could do.

I thought that was a great mindset to have, right? I was in a role and with this elevated thinking process, I was iron-clad tough. Then one day, my right shoulder was dislocated. I remember it well. A significant part of my job was swimming and training in the water. Admittedly, the group of us were doing our usual wrestling/cooling off after our training workout.

Someone looked at me with his head cocked to the side and yelled, "Female! What's wrong with you?" He must've seen the pain on my face. (Stand by for screwed up thinking here.)

Not wanting to draw any undue attention to myself, I merely put my face back in the water and swam (ish) away. I then switched arms for the rest of our training and work that day. There were no tears. Later on, my private healthcare provider put it back in place. I rehabbed as directed, and did my best to keep up with them.

The year continued as years do. There was still plenty of work and swimming. It was my job, what we did. I kept acting like nothing had happened, and I was really good at it. No one seemed to notice that I was now left handed for our workouts and training exercises.

During this time, I became pregnant with our fourth child. Suddenly one day at work, something was very wrong. There was new construction adjacent new to our building and unknowingly the HVAC system was pulling paint fumes into our building. I, and others, became ill. Unfortunately by that time, my total toxic load had become incapacitating.

I don't remember much of the next six weeks. I could not leave my home much because I was very sick. Brain fog as thick as soup often made it hard to put thoughts together. I had to try really hard to focus on what I wanted to say and do. I spent an incredible amount of time on my couch, watching reruns on A &E, drifting off then wonder why the children were *home so soon*, only to realize hours had gone by.

In addition to the emotions that came from growing a baby, mine were seemingly set on *roller coaster*, with no rhyme or reason. Toxins wreaked havoc on my neurotransmitters, having me tearing when I wanted to laugh or suddenly laughing when nothing was funny.

During that time, my body often felt not like it was not my own. It would tingle and twitch and zap. Sometimes it would be strong, then suddenly my left side wouldn't work well, especially my left foot which would drop and trip me. It is hard to explain. Maybe you can relate:

I understand what it is to feel foggy and not be able to walk straight.

I understand what it is to get stuck and can't move.

I have been there.

I want to remind you that tenacity is sewn into our DNA.

I understand, "I'm too tired. Literally. I can't get out of the bed." Because I have been there, too.

I also developed irritant induced asthma. One set of docs wanted me on strong meds, and told me that this brain fog, the neurological issues, and asthma were my *new normal*.

I had three young children and I was pregnant with our fourth. All those little eyes were depending on me. I had a choice in that moment, to continue as I was or prove them wrong and change my story. My decision was that, "If THIS is as good as it gets, THIS is unacceptable."

Instead, I put myself on a journey inward. I asked one question, *What can I control in my life?*

...and explored the answers:

- I could control the chemicals in my house. This would help me breathe better.
- I can control what I put in my face, the foods I eat and the liquid I drink.
- I can control what kind of floor I had. We pulled out all of the carpet.
- I could control the gas stove and got an electric one.

We took out all wheat, sugar, cow's milk, things that were processed, or from a box or can. We ate organic and rotated our foods.

Women, you can overcome layers of problems if you believe in what exists for you on the other side. See, THIS was not going to defeat me.

During all of this, I still didn't cry with intent. In my mind, I was a victim but unwilling to be a victim. I was *going to fight*. I didn't yet understand that by not crying, I was pushing pain into my body and that this resulted in physical disease and discomfort. I didn't yet understand that I had a choice to not fight, to instead listen to my body and hear what it was trying to say.

After about two months of not being able to leave my house, changing my diet, and rearranging most things in my home, I was able to go back to work. Four months later, my 10 lb., 4 oz. bundle of joy was born at home, underwater, to join our family. Most were amazed I continued to work up until the night before she arrived.

When returning to work from postpartum leave, I continued as I had before. I trained hard to catch back up to where I was, to *get my body back*, to prove *pregnancy* and this *chemical thing* wasn't going to change me. I did my work, did my workouts, and taught my classes while pumping milk in my locker room in between.

All was *well* until five months after her birth. During a training evolution, I took an elbow to the face. It fricking hurt like hell, but I wasn't going to quit. Later In the same training evolution, my other shoulder was dislocated. I think it was around then I started to doubt my own belief that I can do anything a man can do. I remember briefly entertaining the thought, "Like, maybe I'm not really cut out for this, and I should just quit." I was sure that I had slipped into the seventh dimension of hell, or something like that, but I wasn't going to quit. AND, I didn't cry.

Now. Listen well. Here's the messed up part. I did not stop the training evolution. I could have. At any time. At any time, I could have said I was done. But I didn't. In MY mind, I could not. I was fighting to prove something, prove that I was good enough and strong enough, and I wasn't going to quit. I ignored my body. I ignored the throbbing in my face and my eye that was swelling. When my left arm wouldn't work, I switched back to using my right one that had been injured 18 months prior.

I was not going to quit and I was not going to let them see me cry. Nope. No crying from this girl. *No crying in boot camp!* That's actually what was often said in jest. So, I swallowed it. And swallowed it. The pain turned into determination and I became surer than ever that I was going to come out of this on top.

The physical pain was there, but mentally I pushed it down. And I didn't stop. Until my safety eventually noticed I wasn't using my left arm. He stopped the evolution and pulled me out of the water because by then I could not get myself out.

Fast forward 14 years.

I had new employment as a manual therapist in a healthcare office. Continuing education is a licensure requirement. I found three classes in a row, 10 days total, which would meet all my requirements. These classes, these techniques, were nothing like I had ever seen. They were soft, gentle. They were slow and patient. And they stirred sensations in my body and memories that I thought I had long forgotten.

Class days consisted of lecture, demo of the techniques, questions, paired practical application of the techniques, more questions. By that last day I was hurting. The sessions were not *hard*, per se, yet my body ached. And in weird places, like my elbows shoulders and wrists, even though, we had not been doing anything that strenuous.

It came time for our first practical of the last day, and my partners asked who wanted to go first. "Me," I raised my hand. I was beat. I needed a nap. I was ready for a rest. Yet, that was not meant to be.

Here is the weird part. As I lay on the table, trying to sleep, not even paying attention to the techniques my partners are doing, I let my mind wander. As they touched different parts of me, for some reason, my thoughts wandered to the pool. I vaguely realized, I was no longer on my back, but laying on my side. My hands are across my chest and I am kicking my legs. I am back there. My body is back there. In the pool. Carrying a brick. Doing side stroke. Training.

The next thing I know, as I am doing pushups in my mind in the pool, I suddenly notice I am also doing them on the table! Counting. In groups of 10. (Some of the best damned pushups I had ever done.)

Back into the my mental pool of water, I grab my brick, swimming on my side, until I roll over and do flutter kicks. And then I'm ON THE TABLE again, counting them out as I had done thousands of times before, "One two three, ONE. One two three, TWO. One two three, THREE. One two three FOUR."

My BODY was in a conference room on a table, yet the memories and energy it held, had me back 14 years to the pool reliving my experiences there.

When it was time to switch places and I had to practice the technique on my fellow student, something truly inspirational happened: My wrists, shoulders, and hands didn't hurt anymore! Actually, I felt pretty good.

What happened to me? Why was I remembering experiences from twelve to fourteen years earlier?

You see, the memories came forward out of my body and into my mind to heal. The stuff was coming up, and boy it was really coming up.

When my brain got out of the way, my body remembered and moved how it needed to move. (We call this Unwinding.) So many times my body had been talking to me, YELLING at me, and I had not been listening. In fact, I thought I was the victim, when in hindsight, the only fight was with myself.

This is the lesson I want you to take away from my story. Every time I thought I was a victim, that I did not have a choice, or that I was *fighting* something, I was confused.

I was not a victim. I DID have a choice. The fight was with myself. Every time I hurt and refused to feel it, every time I refused to cry, I trapped the feelings in my body, in my core. That particular day, I needed the compression through experiencing pushups one more time to start to release what was trapped there.

I needed to re-remember this event so I could get back into my body, to feel it, to cry, to swear. I needed to heal this and I did. It took me that long to bring up the trapped emotions and physical agony, to begin to truly heal it. I needed to do all of those things I was *never allowed* to do. My body responded by releasing the pain it felt, the compensation patterns it was stuck in to protect me. I could almost hear it say, "AH. We can relax now."

The body is amazing. It distributes force and traumas, unconsciously creating patterns to compensate. It remembers them and can form a repeating feedback loop until you consciously make a decision to do something different. Just as I realized I had a choice and made the decision to control what I could control, change my story, and listen to my body, you, too can make the decision to listen to your body. It gives you clues as to which direction you need to take to release the trapped emotion that is causing you physical pain.

Patterns are the driving force in human behavior. Some of them are inherited, some are brought through the DNA and cellular memory, and others are learned through life. Making the decision to disrupt a pattern releases your beautiful body to keep you healthy and happy. It is important to have a self-care routine to ensure you constantly are moving trapped emotions through your body and releasing them.

This is where the terror set in with me for my children. What had I done? I was so dishonorable to my body. My beautiful, strong body that had kept me moving forward. My beautiful, strong body that had helped me grow and care for my babies. My beautiful, strong body that helped me carry other people's bodies, to save lives, yet I ignored it, time and again. What had I done to it? And, what had I been modeling for my children?

As I watched my now assertive high school and college athlete children sustain injury after injury, and attempt to rush back to their sport, I became sickened. They were doing exactly what I taught them! To suck it up. To be tough. To not draw attention to themselves or be a bother; to not let their team down. I was their model, their leader, and I taught them to deny themselves. My heart broke at the realization.

Finally, I cried.

I remember the Easter Sunday when they were all gathered together. I cried as I apologized for doing what I thought was best and realizing the error in my ways.

It took those 10 days of training to show me that my calling was to lead other people to unite their wholeness: Body, mind, and spirit. I get to let them know they have choice, to listen their bodies, in a deeper and compassionate way. They GET to change their story. And to teach them that when they do, when they truly listen and do not just say, "Oh, I have pain", they awaken to their truth and freedom from pain and patterns that no longer serve.

Wellbeing is a choice.

Secret One: Be mindful of your words. You must remove all self-talk that says you are broken, pay attention to the signals your temple is giving you every day. Watch everything you say about your body. Pay attention to the things you say inside of your mind that are never spoken with your mouth.

Secret Two: Starting flow is easy. There are two things you can do to improve your wellbeing now. First, raise your hands up in the air to move energy up and through your body. If that's a challenge, lay on your bed or floor with your arms out to the sides or overhead to open up your chest and abdominal area. Second, use Epsom salts (magnesium sulphate), either in a bath or foot soak. To create a new pattern of self-care energy, pay attention to the foundational supplements (magnesium) and body posture that results in optimal health. *Your body hears you. It wants your attention anytime there is pain or imbalance.*

Secret Three: Write a *Thank You* note. I challenge you to write a thank you note to every part of your body, thanking it for the work it does and has done for you every day. Thank your legs for walking you to your destinations, and your brain for the ideas it generates. Thank your feet for supporting your entire body. Thank your heart for your ability to love and be loved. Showing your body that you love it can help you start to heal even the deepest wounds.

AUTHOR RACHELLE MANIERI

Rachelle is the founder of Reconnecting Your Unlimited Potential, Inc. She is a licensed massage therapist, a myofascial therapist through John Barnes' Myofascial Release, Sedona, AZ, and a Level Three Reiki Practitioner.

She has had the pleasure of working with families and babies as a birth and post-partum doula. She was a peer lactation counselor with the Women Infant Children (WIC) program. She has worked with people of all ages—prenatally to newborns through their 80s.

Rachelle spent two decades coaching and instructing, working with the military and various health care professionals, in Emergency and Rehabilitative Medicine. She continues to work with individuals who have experienced multiple system injuries from barotrauma, concussive trauma, and compression trauma. She interacts with people who live with traumatic brain injuries and post-traumatic stress disorder and their families.

Her experience includes licensed Emergency Medical Technician (EMT), Wilderness Advanced Life Support, Lifeguard and Water Safety Instructor trainer through American Red Cross, physical and aquatic training from The Cooper Institute and United States Navy.

She holds an Associate's of Arts degree in Music and Bachelors of Business in Human Resource Management. She is the mother of four amazing children, one with special needs.

Rachelle is committed to her own personal growth and yours.

She is highly intuitive. She's been on a conscious spiritual journey for many years which has led to deeper understanding of the soul, love, and relationships. Just as with any journey of the soul it doesn't end, it simply and beautifully evolves. She continues to increase her intuitive and energetic awareness through Spiritual Mentorship with Shellie Nelson. Her unique skills and intuitive abilities have allowed her to comfortably interact with people who have varying medical and special needs as well as non-humans, including horses, dogs, and cats.

Connect with the Author. . .

Website: http://www.unlimitedpotentialmfr.com/

"Leadership is the ability to Magically Transform Tragedy into Awesome." ~ Stephanie Leivas

Unlimited Possibilities for Women

STEPHANIE LEIVAS

*H*i there Gorgeous!!! Women in this day and time have taken on a new paradigm; an incredible paradigm that applies to everyone! I grew up with a strong work ethic, taught to me by my father. My father's work ethic was hard and limited. Females in our family could not express themselves openly without consequences. This upbringing both jaded me and empowered me to move my life into alignment and belief in unlimited possibilities.

My mother told me to find a rich man to take care of me. And so I married men who were rich—as well as controlling and mentally abusive. Today I create programs that help women see unlimited possibilities in their lives, and how to steer clear of future train-wreck relationships.

Women have had limitations placed subconsciously upon them for as long as time has existed. Many of the limitations, many of the glass ceiling moments, are expansions of old beliefs that are no longer relevant. Young girls now have more opportunities than ever to only excel, to be victorious in work, and in life. There are no glass ceilings when we support and encourage one another to be and do more in our own lives.

Money and Love are two areas where I see women most often stumble and fall.

We have been taught for so long that wanting money is bad. Truth is, your money situation is drawn by your energy and your abundance beliefs, programs that you agreed to, aligned with, and bought and sold to yourself as true in your reality.

Our mothers and their mothers and their mothers before taught us a falsehood that they bought into: that it is required to find love. The truth is, love is within oneself, whether solo or with a partner.

I am becoming an Energy Master and am excited to create new programs for women who want a deeper healing of their wounds. The pain that women hold onto is heartbreaking. Working with energy is a magical and invisible work, but the results are life-altering and mind-blowing. The Universe has given me a gift of knowing who people are at their core level of humanity. Through their Akashic record, I can pinpoint past life experiences that are begging to be healed.

I was diagnosed with Multiple Sclerosis twelve years into my previous marriage. Because I lived a life following patterns I did not own, I was not being true to myself. Through my energy work, I have come to believe that mental illness results in the physical manifestation of illness in the body. Because I didn't know how to fully and completely love myself, my body shut down on me.

Has this ever happened to you? Have you ever been in an emotional situation that almost at once resulted in a physical disparity?

My husband walked out on me one day after I found out I had MS. Maybe this was the Universe signaling me to slow down and re-evaluate my life. I took this as a sign that it was time for me to awaken to who I had become and who I wanted to be.

I made a promise to myself that I would become unlimited in me! By making this decision, I capped off my firm intention to go as deep inside of my soul as possible and find the way out of the relentless feedback loop my life had become.

I learned about soul re-alignment, integration, and past-life re-gression. I learned how to discover my patterns and find out why those patterns were as they were. I was able to gently make the shifts I needed to get back on my feet.

I made a decision to do what I desired to do—to help other women become aligned with their awesomeness and make choices that make them feel bliss and joy. I started my own business as an Advanced Soul Realignment Akashic Records Intuitive. I believe that no one has to get sick and that I can help them heal. I believe that knowing where you came from, the history of your lineage and the karmic path you took on at birth, all help you be the best version of yourself.

When I first decided to follow this path, I encountered many mo-ments where I fell into self-doubt. I would have inner conversations that went something like these:

I can't do this because I am sick. When you have a disabling condition that causes extreme pain in your body, it is very easy to use this ex-cuse.

I don't have the tools to succeed. I don't have my website, or a store-front, or an email list. Do you know this one? There are tools every-where.

This is going to be very difficult. When you are very sick, it's easy to see difficulty and not ease. However, if you can live it and dream it, you can have it.

I am a victim. This one sneaks up in every interaction. Feeling that someone or something is responsible for your lack of happiness, is the number one excuse women make.

I need to take care of everyone else and when they are ok, I will begin. This is part of motherhood, but it is also something women must re-lease to grow.

I am too fat. Believe it or not, this is an unspoken fear of many women who want to get themselves out there.

Fat is fabulous. So is thin. We are all in this together. It's difficult for me today to realize how often I said these things, to myself and aloud to people. Now I have broken free from saying those things. Breaking out of negative self-talk is one of the most challenging changes a woman can take on, and I am no exception.

Having MS taught me that I am normal, I am broken. I was in shock when I got diagnosed with MS. My life changed and this diagnosis became the cornerstone of my ability to move forward with what I love to do. Today, I know this to be true: I am unbroken and I am free from limitations.

You can make changes in your life. Dig deep into yourself and be honest. Always congratulate yourself for even the smallest things.

I thank my body every time I can walk a little further, or the leg spasms stop. I know how to just be me with no apologies! I have learned to lead my own ship through the MS and through having loving conversations with my body. man at a time.

AUTHOR STEPHANIE LEIVAS

Connect with the Author. . .

Social Media

Facebook: https://www.facebook.com/advancedsoulrealignment/

"Because true belonging only happens when we present our authentic, imperfect selves to the world, our sense of belonging can never be greater than our level of self-acceptance." ~ Brene Brown, Phd

Social Media's Impact on Leadership

KAVITA C. MELWANI

As a mother, wife, and entrepreneur, at any given time I usually manage multiple projects. I have a strong desire to raise happy and healthy boys who are also good people. As a Women's Empowerment Coach, I support women to ignite their self-confidence and self-worth so they can succeed on their own terms. Often the goals and standards that I set for myself create a level of self-induced stress. In addition to this combination of internal and external stressors, being active on social media adds another dimension.

When clients come to me they are often confused, lost, or feel like they are going down the wrong path and don't know what to change. They don't know what to do or in what order. There is often a lack of focus to the actions they take.

The first thing we work on together is clarifying their vision, which is what their inner voice calls them to do. If they are in alignment with their vision, they can live a joyous, fulfilling life.

As I work with people on clarifying their vision, it is often hard for them to discern the voices that come from their childhood, spouses, friends, and media. Social media adds to the already complex influences, creating for many of my clients, layers of both stress and confusion that are challenging to unwrap.

Social Media has been a life changing outlet for many people. Businesses have been formed and flourished using social media. I especially appreciate stories about people who have been able to get in touch with long lost friends. Adding to these benefits is the greater sense of perceived connection.

And yet, along with the many positive impacts, there is a shadow side to social media. As my clients work to clarify their vision, the concerns of their friends' opinions expressed on social media often contribute to their confusion.

It is common to have an incomplete picture of what the lives of our peers on social media truly are because, by design, social media paints a limited picture. The mundane aspect of daily life, the work it takes to succeed, and the reality behind selfies attached to a rosy post is often more complex and much less exciting, not as fun and definitely less adventurous than it seems. People use social media as a way to connect but in many ways, it can leave them disconnected because it puts another mask between them and others.

Social media connections are often made on a superficial level. The amount of posts and shares that are authentic are few, and far in between. The pictures of the social events, selfies, and vacation shares often leave us comparing our own lives to the posts. We question why our vacations are not as fun, or we wonder why we aren't going on as many vacations as others. I counsel my clients, and remind my-self as well, that the selfies are posed and taken using the best angles and often edited with one of the countless photo editing apps available.

Although most women I work with know that social media is a snippet of life and is truly a facade of what people want you to now, it still affects their decisions. Exposure to social media can create a slow river of doubt in their minds, causing them to question whether their lives are enough, which in turn means they are not enough. In reality, all these posts are a reflection of human beings searching for validation. We all need to be seen and heard. Social media can help us feel this for a short time, at least until the next post.

If we continue posting the way we do now women will continue to question how others look so much happier, younger, and more successful. How do others seem to have it all together? Women internally question whether something is wrong with them.

In our disconnected society, it is vital that we choose to be authentic. The display of mistakes and our humanity are all vital so that we can connect on a deeper level. If we continue to stay connected using social media as our only source of human connection, we will continue to feel less than, feel lonely, and even feel as if there is something wrong with us and our lives.

Authenticity is not the sharing of the deepest, darkest secrets. It is not sharing that our lives are terrible. Authenticity is simply showing up on social media as a human being. Authenticity is posting the string of vacation pictures *and* sharing our struggles. Being authentic means you speak your truth despite it seeming unpopular.

How do we become more authentic in our social media activity? It's time to say things like,

I am confused about what to do about _____.

I am stressed because _____.

Of course, I am always an advocate for using your intuition to determine the appropriate time and place to express your truth. Choose your audience wisely.

Keeping secrets and the truth under wraps takes up energy and time. It prevents us from feeling connected and denies the satisfaction of being seen and heard and providing that connection for others.

I remember how afraid I was to speak my truth about how tired and stressed I was with two young children. It seemed like everyone around me had it all together and kept repeating how wonderful being a mother was and how they were so happy staying at home with their kids. Other moms would talk about their recipes for organic homemade baby food, and how they easily lost all their baby weight.

In the meantime, I could barely function with bottled baby food and really needed a break. When I finally chose to break down and tell another mom how I felt, the floodgates opened. It was like I made it OK to love your kids and also not love every aspect of being a mom. That conversation was amazing! I felt more connected and I know the other mom did, too.

What if we choose a way to communicate that unites?

What if we communicate authentically?

What if we share our heart with a carefully selected few?

How would life change for women—for you—if we support each other publicly and privately?

Will you answer these questions and make the changes? We *can* do it together, one powerful woman at a time.

AUTHOR KAVITA C. MELWANI, M.ED

CERTIFIED WOMEN'S EMPOWERMENT COACH

Kavita empowers women all over the world to achieve their goals and live on purpose. Her methodologies include: Coaching, Hypnosis, Regression, Meditation, Reiki, and a wide range of additional energetic and spiritual tools.

Kavita is committed to help women improve their self-worth and to move past overwhelm, stress, and anxiety so they can live joyous and prosperous lives.

Connect with the Author. . .

Website: www.heartandsoulbusiness.info
Social Media
Facebook: https://www.facebook.com/groups/connectedentrepreneurs/

"Being a leader is leading by example; nurturing, guiding, and coaching, giving of yourself to the teams' success." ~ Marie Dahl

Lead by Nature. Lead by Default, Lead with Compassion

MARIE DAHL

Growing up on a farm in a rural community presents many opportunities to be a Leader. I can thank my mother and grandmother for instilling leadership in me at an early age. My roots are grounded in the concept of female leadership. In my area, often times you see women in volunteer positions.

These are important roles as they are much needed for the success of programs that help everyone. Many people benefit from the contribution of these women, yet they are undervalued for what they do to support the community. So many of the women whom I see working in volunteer positions, and generally helping anyone and everyone, never talk about the work they do.

In our society, we are led to believe women should be active only in these volunteer roles. Society also often undervalues the strong leadership skills that are the backbone of this kind of volunteerism.

Women see a need and fill a need. Our compassion and loyalty shines through in all areas of our life's journey. We are teachers, healers and caregivers to the world, yet we remain unnoticed as leaders.

Leadership through the lens of retail management

As a Manager in retail we are always looking for great competencies, or areas where we can work on these competencies, to build a Leader. A few of the qualities we look for in our staff will show you how the retail establishment views leadership qualities.

- Acting with Integrity and Building Trust
- Face Challenges Head On
- Ability to Direct and Follow Through
- Not afraid to take a stand
- Build and keep confidence high
- Admit their mistakes
- Make decisions based on the team
- Ensure credit and praise are given when merited
- Teachers and Guides by Default
- Team Builders

Leaders give of themselves for the good of the team. A leader is only as good as the team they have helped build. If the team fails, the leader fails. If the team wins, the Leader needs to be humble and call out the successes of the team players.

Women are Family Leaders by Nature

We truly are *Conceived to Lead* by virtue of our appointment to be mothers, grandmothers, and matriarchs. In the family, we lead in many ways. My mother and grandmother taught me real values that I have used my whole life to be a leader making problematic decisions.

Leadership truly begins in the home. Leading our families, we often put ourselves in supporting roles and do not think we are leaders. We consistently under value what we bring to the table when we support our families our friends. We are light houses of hope when some- one needs another person to lean on. We inspire our children and our grandchildren. We become strong in our darkest hours. We dig deep within ourselves to find the strength to get through whatever journey we are on. We help, support, and encourage. We take clear the path and take on others burdens to lighten someone else's load.

Leading without realizing we are leading.

We lead by example. We shine bright even when we under value ourselves. When we are in a coaching role, many women do not truly realize that they are being a leader. One never knows who we are in- spiring or giving hope to. We just do these things naturally, without much thought, because we see the need and we fill the need.

Leadership knows no age.

I know younger women who have inspired me and taught me. They have led me to become a better person, a better leader myself. Posi- tive influences from positive women of all ages and from all stops along the path of life have helped me to be a better leader. Without their hard work and efforts, there would not be success.

Leaders shine a light on others great ideas and opinions. A great leader will always be open to learning no matter the age of the person teaching. Leaders know the value of involving people in the planning of a goal. A team involved at all stages of a project will have a better buy-in and commitment to the success of the project.

Leaders build up their people, encourage them to make decisions, and help them by coaching along the way.

Leaders share the bigger picture.

They share the whys. Leaders share how all the different pieces of the puzzle will fit together in the end. Leaders help their teams drive for the results that are needed to achieve their goals. Leaders have a strong drive to accomplish goals and exceed the expectations. Leaders see the possibilities. They seek out the opportunities. Leaders help their teams drive the execution of the plan. They work to build up their teams. When the leader is down in the trenches working alongside the team, putting in the sweat equity along with their team members, this effort builds relationships and trust among team members and in their team leaders.

Leaders are skilled at seeing potential talent in people and are willing to invest themselves and time into that person to build them up and develop them into the potential that the leader sees. Leaders have candid conversations with their team members to find out what their goals are, to share the big picture, and identify the vision they have for themselves. Wanting something for someone when they do not want that at all, will not work.

A leader keeps an open mind to the feedback coming from the team members and recognizes that frank and effective communications, and more importantly listening, are super important in a person's role as a leader.

Leaders lead their business with a vision and a strategic plan. Leaders will use their broad thinking to expand their boundaries. Leaders are always talking about possibilities and always creating a picture of the future. Leaders ensure their teams understand the vision and the final goal.

Together the team creates and establishes plans to achieve the steps towards the end goal. Each step is an accomplishment on the path to the end goal. Leaders step in and guide and coach their teams along the way, removing obstacles in the way of accomplishing the goal at hand.

Leaders take the fails of the team players and turn those into coaching and learning moments. A leader will ask what did you learn from this failed attempt. How can we change this into a win? Much like teaching a child to walk—you must crawl and fall before you walk. Leaders need to be able to pick up their team members dust them off and help them to try again.

Whether the team needs their hands held or are ready to jump up and say, "I can do this!", a leader is there for understands that each person is unique, and will adjust their teaching to suit who they are coaching. We all have different learning styles and that's ok. A great Leader sees that, and they figure out a way that they can help that person to the best of their abilities. Through team differences greatness grows. When encouraged and respected, everyone benefits and learns from those differences.

Leaders embody humility and respect. An effective leader is confident but not arrogant; they are humble and show mutual respect and caring. They ensure they are approachable as well as likeable. But at the same time, they are not pushovers. They take pride in the growth of the team and the contributions of each team member. Every team has differences as well as similarities and good leaders respect that. A leader must be engaging and approachable they should show they are vulnerable and make mistakes as well. Because acting with integrity is key in having the respect of your team.

If you do not respect your Leader because of an integrity issue it will be impossible for you to fully commit to that leader. You will always look at them and think about the time they did not keep their integrity in place. You will also wonder what else has happened that you do not know about.

When a leader takes a risk as a way to achieve a positive goal with the potential for great results, and fails at the goal, it's important to admit to the fail. A leader takes time to see what can be learned from this lesson to turn the fail into a win—if not this time, then the next.

A leader will take a fail and turn it into a coaching moment, a learning experience. They will dust themselves off and move forward yet again, with new knowledge gained from the experience; knowledge to be passed onto future team members.

If your team feels appreciated and valued, they will work harder. Thanking someone for a job well done puts a smile on their face. Calling out a job well done and recognizing the value of their part in front of others means even more when the rest of the team get to congratulate them as well.

Just showing up adds no value. Excelling and pushing yourself beyond your own personal limits is where the gratification comes into play. Leaders think on their feet. When they see a challenge coming or find an obstacle, they quickly think of ways to overcome that issue.

Master minding with a few key people is a sign of a great leader who gives team members a chance to put their ideas forward. Each team member grows through the master mind sessions and leaders mold ideas and solutions by asking questions, gathering input and insights, and fostering the growth of the team.

Sometimes, through the sharing of stories or experiences, accomplishments and mistakes, new ideas grow. Leaders listen and figure out how to combine individual ideas to make the greatest plan to follow. No one is perfect, we are always learning and growing. Leaders must be open to learn, grow, and change. Nothing stays the same. Everything is constantly evolving.

I have held many Leadership roles from running restaurants to bar lounges but most of my years have been spent in retail management. I have always believed we need to build each other up, encourage growth, and work towards the dream goal. Celebrate each other's successes, be happy. Be the lighthouse for someone you do not even know is watching you.

AUTHOR MARIE DAHL

Marie Dahl is the author of *The Adventures of Aksana the Shy Fairy* and has authored poem in a coffee table book called *Blue Birds Song*.

While pursuing her career in retail management for over 20 years, Marie has led many people into management roles, coaching and mentoring them along the way. During this same time, she was a single Mom to three children, two daughters and a son and now enjoys spoiling three grandsons who are the light of her heart.

Marie created books in the series, *The Adventures of Aksana the Shy Fairy,* to celebrate the birthday of Aksana, her niece's daughter. Aksana was born on the same day as Marie and also Great Grandpa George Pronych.

Connect with the Author. . .

Social Media
Facebook: http://www.facebook.com/mariedahl
Twitter: http://www.twitter.com/asksanatheshyfairy
Twitter :@AksanaShy
Instagram: http://www.instagram.com/asksanatheshyfairy
Email: Aksanatheshyfairy@gmail.com

"The essence of great leadership is the desire that those you lead achieve more than yourself." ~ *Coni K Meyers*

Are You a Kickbutt Leader?

CONI K MEYERS

*N*apoleon Hill, author of, Think and Grow Rich, accepted Andrew Carnegie's 20-year challenge to, without any kind of compensation, interview all the world leaders Carnegie knew. Andrew Carnegie told Hill that there would be times when he would feel like quitting. When that happened, he should look in a mirror and imagine he was talking to Carnegie and say, "I'm not only going to equal your achievements in life, but I'm going to challenge you at the post and pass you at the grandstand."

The essence of great leadership is the desire that those you lead achieve more than yourself that they pass *you* at the grandstand.

A good leader is there to support and steer the ship in the direction of a clear vision that their team can buy into and embrace as their own.

We have all met leaders who do not understand this concept and believe leadership is about telling people what to do. As women, we are naturally nurturing, compassionate, and enjoy collaboration. We appreciate consensus when a decision is made, thus making us all leaders and *Conceived to Lead*. We only need to own it and step into it.

My childhood was spent on a farm in Nebraska. As a small child, I made a deal with my younger brother: if he would play dolls and dress-up with me, then I would play trucks with him. I also convinced my visiting cousins to follow me around the farm doing what I told them to do, which occasionally resulted in mischief and parental consequences. OK, so maybe I didn't use my leadership skills for the betterment of others then but I certainly improved my negotiation skills!

I was married at 19 and divorced with three children at 23 and working as a service clerk for a car dealership. I quickly advanced from office manager to becoming a business manager for a dealership with five facilities. By then I had remarried and my husband was offered a position in Los Angeles, so off we went to California. I was hired as general manager for a small Italian import company but my management style didn't fit with the culture of the business. I was not happy but wasn't sure what to do about it since we had just moved to LA. Had I known of the leadership techniques I now use, my team and I would have enjoyed a better work environment.

I was contemplating leaving one Friday afternoon, when the company health insurance agent (a thorn in my side) called to ask, "Do you know anyone interested in a sales career?"

Laughing I said, "Selling insurance? Sure, I have a couple of enemies to send you."

That weekend my family was headed to the mountains for a little getaway. I mentioned to my husband how unhappy I was, and about the insurance agent's phone call. I told him that I thought I might be interested in sales so we agreed I would give him a call and find out more about the position.

On Monday morning, I gave the agent a call back to ask if the sales position was still open. After all the grief I had given him over the years, he got even by telling me that there was a secretarial position available. Yow! Did that send me off! I told him I wasn't interested in a secretarial position. He put me on hold for at least five minutes (it seemed like an hour). When he came back on the phone, he recited my own words back to me, quotes of things I had said to him in the past that made him believe I would make a good salesperson. He knew that if he had asked directly if I was interested in sales, my answer would have been an emphatic NO. Instead, he asked a question that would make me stop, think, and imagine, "Would this be a good fit for me?" I've since come to learn this is a technique that John Maxwell refers to as the *Law of the Buy-In*.

Nine months later I was Rookie of the Year for Metropolitan Life Insurance and one of the highest paid new agents in the company.

Sadly, I saw firsthand that my story was not always repeated among agents. I recall when a successful securities agent came into the office and quit. He had a different sales manager who was not good at supporting and helping his team. It really bothered me that this agent was a quality sales person who felt he had to quit because he was not getting the help he needed to be successful.

As a result, I wrote a letter to the Regional Manager. I explained that, in my opinion, the reason there was such a high turnover of quality individuals was because management was putting people into the position of sales manager who were not good leaders. In the letter I called it, "Peter's Principle Personified." I cited the example of the sales manager who had not been a quality sales person or leader with his clients. Thus, when he became a sales manager, he did not have the tools to become a good leader for his sales agents.

After receiving the letter, the Regional Manager called me and asked if I would be willing to put my money where my mouth was. I said yes. They assigned me to a sales team that was number 48 out of the 49 teams in the Western Region. Needless to say, I had a lot of work to do. Never having been afraid of a challenge, in nine months we worked our way out of that position to number three AND we added eight additional agents.

Why am I telling you this story? It reveals a few components of good leadership. Our company health insurance agent, who became my sales manager, observed that I was not one to back down and stood up for what was right. He saw that I was organized, tenacious, and had good follow-up. Under his mentoring I learned by his example how to serve my clients and to be a good leader supporting their needs. He had not been Rookie of the Year, but he encouraged, and in fact wanted, me to pass him in the grandstands

At that time, I was one of a handful of female insurance agents and when I became a Sales Manager in the Western Region, I was the only female sales manager. I was 27 years of age with three mature men on my sales force and one female. The men were close to retirement and were biding their time, waiting for that day to come. The one woman agent on my team was on welfare.

I faced challenges right away. The men didn't believe that a woman, and a young woman at that, would be able to help them. They would not even come into my office and sit down. I knew I had to win them over. I began by taking them on sales calls with me. It was a slow-going strategy, and it worked. Once they experienced my selling and serving methods, they recognized why I had great success.

In time, I recruited several women and another man to enlarge my team and eventually everyone on my team affectionately called me their 'manageress'.

In the 1980s, the nation's workplace had a serious problem with sexual harassment. Any working woman from that period will confirm that sexual remarks, offers of affairs, and other degrading humiliations were common. My last straw with Metropolitan occurred during a nationwide company contest where I and six other men won.

The competitor that I am, I pressed myself and my team to work around the clock including weekends. Little did I know the award was a nice men's cardigan sweater. When I asked for a woman's cardigan, I was told to give the sweater to my husband. Yow! Again. I told them that my husband didn't win the contest that I won it. Then I quit.

My manager helped me buy into his clear vision of an ethical, quality salesperson. His support was provided by word and example and I did my best to imitate him with my own team. When growing my team, I looked for persons with qualities that I knew would make them great sales people. I strove to bring out their best while they grew as great agents who served their clients well.

In the 80s, leadership was somewhat dictatorial. Today, leadership is regarded as a supporting collaborative role. As a leader, we give our best and when we move on, we leave the position in a better place than when we stepped into it. There are great financial benefits for individuals and businesses when leadership is conducted with respect for the team members, helping individuals to grow their skills, and empowering them to lead.

In a 2011 study by Harvard Business Review, a team of universities, research firms, psychologists, and neuroscientists evaluated top level executives from 57 different sectors of business and divided them into two groups. All were put through a battery of tests. One group was placed in an eight-week mindfulness leadership training program and the other group was not. Twelve weeks after the training had ended every leader was re-tested. The group going through mindfulness training was found to have actually enlarged the gray matter of their brains. It was also found that through these practices there was an astounding 80 percent increase in their resilience, collaboration, and agility in handling complex problems and situations.

The results of these studies have had a large impact on leadership training. My own leadership abilities grew as I began to use these techniques and share them with others. Over the years I have helped thousands of individuals and businesses achieve sales and marketing success. Now I help individuals and businesses adapt and integrate these leadership techniques to all aspects of their lives and businesses. It is gratifying to follow their growth and share their success as they see their own leadership skills expand.

You can learn these same techniques that I teach. Here are five practices that you can start today:

1. Before starting your work day, take 10 minutes in your office or before you get out of the car to clear your mind. Breathe, meditate, envision your day. When you center yourself, and get out of auto pilot, you will find problems are much more easily solved, others that you need to deal with will respond more favorably, and that your creative mind will open up to offer better solutions.

2. Do not start your day by looking at social media or reading emails. Research has proven that we lose ten percent of our IQ if we do this first thing in the morning. Instead, be clear about what the outcome of the day will be. Then do I what I call sensorize it. What does it look, smell, taste, sound and feel like? When you can see it clearly all you need to do is step into it.

3. When you are about to go to a meeting or have a difficult conversation, take two minutes to breathe before stepping into the meeting or starting the conversation. Once you center yourself imagine what the outcome is that you want so you have a clear picture when you start the conversation.

4. Help others to be present by asking something personal. Showing that you care about them personally engages that person and brings them to the present moment. It is important to acknowledge them before asking something of a person. And to be authentic about your acknowledgement.
One high level executive I interviewed initiated a book club with her team. Before she starts a strategic planning meeting, they discuss the book for five minutes, which helps to bring everyone to the meeting mentally and not just physically. She finds that the meetings are much more productive, last a shorter period, and the creative juices flow more easily.

5. On your way home from the office, do NOT turn on the car radio. Turn OFF your cellphone, clear your mind and breathe for 10 minutes. This will prepare you for your family and friends so that you can be present for them.

I recently interviewed Dr. Bernice Ledbetter, EdD, Director for the Center for Women in Leadership at Pepperdine University. I asked her to share one practice that she uses. Her response may surprise you. When she is part of an event where people come together to collaborate, she brings a chime and initiates mindfulness meditation. While she doesn't always refer to it as meditation, she believes that this practice is useful and that it's important to find a way to sustain ourselves. Today, everything happens at such a fast pace that it is easy to forget who we are.

To break your glass ceiling, you must be present, you must have a clear vision of the outcome you expect, and you must surround yourself with others who share your vision. Use your God given gifts of nurturing, compassion, and collaboration. Create the vision and practice these kickbutt leadership techniques to be the best leader you can be.

AUTHOR CONI K MEYERS, LMC CBLC, CDC

My past consisted of a life philosophy of *Work, Work, Work...play*. In my old life, I was involved in taking two companies from the local market to the national stage. I also owned four separate consulting firms. I have been recognized with numerous awards and designations in my 35 years of helping thousands of individuals and businesses.

Six years ago, my husband passed away only four days after we celebrated our 25th wedding anniversary. This was my brick wall as Oprah describes it. I love the way Oprah talks about those times in our lives when God is trying to direct us in the direction we are supposed to be going.

She says, "First you are hit with a pebble, then a rock, then a boulder and then a brick wall."

God was trying to get me on track with my life's purpose. I tried to return to my old life, but when I would have a conversation with my partners or clients, it was like I was having an out-of-body experience. It just didn't work.

I found that the *Work, Work, Work...play* philosophy that I had lived by was not something that my heart could get back into. I knew that I needed to find something that gave me a new purpose...a new passion. I wanted to know why I was put on this earth. I now refer to this as a *Crystalline Moment*. I began to realize that I not only wanted to work and make money, but I also wanted to have fun and to give back. That created my new life philosophy of *Have Fun, Give Back, Make Money* in that order. I can assure anyone reading this it is a much better philosophy.

I had to do what I tell others to do. I had to stop, reflect, and determine why I was put on this earth. What was my purpose...my why? Crystalline means sparkly or clear so Crystalline Moments are moments of clarity. I started looking at my life and realized there were moments that had affected my life for over 50 years. I started examining those as well as many other Crystalline Moments that happened after my husband passed. I realized that these moments are put in our path to direct us into our purpose. Each moment helped me step closer into my destiny. Now I am living the life I was put on this beautiful earth to live and enjoy being of service to others. When you look at your own moments, no matter how difficult or how wonderful they are, you will find the opportunity for your life as well.

My greatest joy now is watching others turn their dreams into their destiny. That starts with our personal leadership skills and vision. I am most proud of my international best-selling book *Crystalline Moments* as it is being read and shared all around the world. It is helping people discover the opportunities their own moments are creating, and helping them step into their purpose, their destiny. I am working on a series of *Crystalline Moment* books that will be devoted to leadership, both personally and professionally. My other two best-selling books are *The Success Chronicles* and *Resilience in the Storm*.

In the last six years, I have added to my 35 years of experience and credentials. I am a John Maxwell Certified Business and Leadership Coach, a Certified Dreambuilder Coach, and I am most proud of my Life Mastery Consultant Certification. (It is similar to having a master's degree in life coach training.)

I offer a number of training courses, retreats, workshops, and personal coaching. My exclusive S.O.L.V.E. program is how to... *Create true Success by discovering your Opportunities through great Leadership, Vision and Engagement.* This is a five-module program which can be taken individually or all together. The leadership component I call *Kickbutt Leadership.* This module teaches 12 practices and techniques that will make you a better leader personally and professionally.

My retreats serve the attendees and always include giving back to others. My last retreat in Mexico affected over 250 lives. Whether it is a small intimate retreat in my backyard or a large international retreat, everyone participating is a part of my *Give Back* philosophy.

I founded the Crystalline Moments Success Movement to bring people together to share their moments of clarity in both their personal or professional lives. What better way to change the world than changing our lives and in turn changing the lives around us. I love the difference that is being made by people who read my books and the people I meet and serve.

Connect with the Author. . .

Website: www.conimeyers.com
Social Media
Facebook: https://www.facebook.com/conikmeyers/
LinkedIn: https://www.linkedin.com/in/conimeyers
Email: Coni@ConiMeyers.com

"Leadership means you are one conversation away from changing someone's life forever." ~ Annette Marie Moore

Confident in Her Shoes

ANNETTE MARIE MOORE

*D*id you know you are one conversation away from changing someone's life forever? That's a bold statement, isn't it?

Have you ever thought about all the powerful leaders in your life who have changed your life?

What about the not so powerful people?

I've had a lot of people influence me when I was younger, but dwelled on the negative people and their misdeeds that impacted my life. I let fear control my life, and I missed out on opportunities.

I have not always been confident in my own shoes: The confidence I have today is a result of ignoring bullies and overcoming health issues, driven by my desire to help women live a wholehearted, healthy lifestyle. The purpose of my story is to show you how a skinny, shy, and unconfident girl from Ohio overcame obstacles and paved the way to become a successful entrepreneur.

My Childhood

Growing up in Ohio, I was one of four siblings. My brothers and I were active in sports; however, my sister liked to read a lot. I really admired my sister; things seemed to come easy for her! I also loved to eat, but I was a picky eater who ate weird food. I liked bologna with mashed up potato chips and mayonnaise on white bread. I loved to eat anchovies on my pizza because my dad ate anchovies. I even won a lemon eating contest at a local park. Weird, right? I didn't eat a lot of sweets or drink many sodas, they were reserved for special occasions, a pizza night or holidays. (I don't drink sodas anymore, because they hurt my stomach and caused migraines, too.)

Faith is the Foundation of My Leadership

My faith is important to me. It placed me on solid footing as a child and has become even more integral to my life today. Born and raised a Catholic, I now call myself a Christian. Faith is the foundation of my life and the reason I am a leader. Faith and running go hand in hand; they have impacted my life forever.

Running Track and Enjoying Life

Succumbing to peer expectations, I became a cheerleader in middle school. I wanted to hang out with my friends and wear makeup, so I joined the squad. I especially liked running track, and I also played volleyball and soccer.

My main sport focus of my childhood was running. I started running at the age of nine. I ran track, short distances mostly. People called me Speedy Gonzales because I was fast and small. I won many awards and even excelled at hurdles, javelin, discus, relay races, and race walking. I also ran cross country. I enjoyed everything but long-distance running. In my twenties, much to my surprise, long-distance running became my true passion and still is today.

From elementary school to high school, I also ran for a local city team called the Mound City Dashers. I even started running road races at an early age. When I was 12, I ran a turkey trot with my Mom. We had to guess the time for a mile race that we thought we could run. The person who guessed the closest time won first place. Guess what? I won! I was interviewed by a reporter who published my story in a local newspaper. That was a big deal for only being 12 years old.

The headline read, "Dasher beats prediction for mile...West Carrollton girl, 12 needs little excuse to take off running."

Another article featured a photo of my friend and I race walking. (Yes, that is a sport. It was popular in the late 70s.) The caption read "Helen Lutz, Annette Gonzales show determination in finishing a mile walk."

Only thing I could think of was, "Hey, they spelled my last name wrong in the newspaper."

Another accomplishment occurred when my two brothers and I were interviewed and had our photos taken by Sports Illustrated. They were doing an article about sports-minded families. We didn't get featured in the story, but I still have the photos. I wasn't bothered too much by not getting in the magazine because I had braces on my teeth at the time.

From all the local newspaper clippings I had saved, my name was featured in the local newspaper at least 51 times. There may have been more, but I stopped counting. I earned many trophies, medals, and ribbons but unfortunately most of them were stolen in a house burglary.

My years involved in sports were a time in my life where I felt confident in my ability to have a victory when I wanted it badly enough.

Leading Through the Pain

My life has certainly transitioned since the time of my childhood and teenage years. Being physically active, my love for cooking, and eating healthy have been assets throughout my adult life. I've taught men's aerobics, worked with several personal trainers, and worked as a medical assistant in a doctor's office. A few years ago, I participated in a 30-day fitness challenge at my gym to lose weight or body fat. Guess what? I had fun participating in the challenge, met some new friends, and I lost the most body fat! I won $ 600 and earned a BMI of 19. A BMI of 18.5 to 24.9 is the best healthy range for young and middle aged female adults, without being underweight.

I continue to run road races and recently participated in my first 3.1-mile obstacle course mud race. It was wet, muddy, and challenging, but so much fun! My fitness goals are to run a duathlon, triathlon, half marathon, and marathon within the next year. I am in the best shape of my life and I am confident in my running shoes.

I've talked to many people over the years regarding their poor health. I've also had a lot of women ask me about my secrets to good health. I frequently gave away free health secrets, but I never thought I should or would be making that a business.

So many women today are neither active nor eat healthy. They work the typical nine to five or are busy raising a family, or both; often neglecting themselves in the process. I understand, I was a single mom raising my daughter juggling life's rewards and challenges. I encourage you today to walk, run, or simply be more active; wriggle your butt...move every day! Every step counts towards a healthier you!

The reason I do what I do today is because I saw so many unhealthy senior citizens with chronic diseases when I was a medical assistant at a doctor's office. I want to do something to change the way American women live; healthy wife, healthy life. Right? As an added benefit, women can share their health secrets with their families.

According to projections from the Center for Disease Control, by 2020 three out of four deaths will be caused by cancer, heart disease, and diabetes. The CDC also states that 75 percent of all chronic diseases are preventable with proper lifestyle choices. So why is the typical American Diet so unhealthy? And what can we do about it?

I hear many women complain about their looks, their weight, and health issues. I recognize their suffering and empathize with their feeling of defeat. The short of it is, a lot of women are emotional eaters; when things get stressful or they get depressed, they turn to sugar, or any comfort food, and overeat. You have probably offed an entire carton of ice-cream in your lifetime, honestly everyone has their own comfort food of choice. Happy to say, I don't eat bologna sandwiches or anchovies anymore, but I still love my lemons!

Women can easily gain ten, twenty, or thirty-plus pounds that can turn into a chronic disease. Dieting can be a temporary fix. As old, bad habits return, most gain the weight back. It takes a short amount of time to gain the weight and can take three times the amount of time to lose the weight. In overeating through emotional trouble, women consume a lot of gluten and sugar, tossing their hormones and metabolism into a frenzy. It's a vicious cycle.

I serve women by educating them, providing resources, and inspiring them to get rid of the Diet mentality and adopt A Wholehearted Healthy Lifestyle! A diet is temporary, but a lifestyle is the rest of your life! Poor health, erratic emotions, and low self-esteem are all connected. Once you find the solutions, take action to become confident in your shoes!

Being Confident in My Shoes

As a high-school student I was bullied. I would say I was fit and in shape as I worked hard to achieve my results. Skinny was a word bullies used to bring me down and cause me to lose self-confidence. The stress associated with the bullying caused me to dabble with bouts of bulimia and anorexia. I felt there was peer pressure to look beautiful and be popular.

I was even bullied as an adult. Can you believe it? Sometimes this pressure was unbearable. Leadership is the ability to help your sisters rise after trauma. If you have been bullied or suffered health issues and it impacted your adult life, feel free to reach out to me.

I was mocked because I was small. People can be so cruel and yes, skinny girls get bullied, too. People who are hurt will hurt others; when

I felt burdened, I simply ran. It was my emotional release and my connection to God; still is today.

Cruel comments took an occasional toll on my ability to believe in myself. Some say there is a direct connection among emotions, physical illness, and self-esteem. I truly believe it; I'm a prime example. As an adult, I have chosen to forgive people who bullied me, or hurt me. Living in unforgiveness can cause health issues. I say No to bullies.

As a result of holding myself accountable, I overcame anorexia, bulimia, anemia, fibromyalgia, fibroids, hormone imbalances, PTSD, asthma, and torn ligaments. I continue to be self-aware of my food allergies and gluten intolerance. Pain and loss have been powerful motivators in transforming my life. And can transform your life too!

When I couldn't physically run due to an ailment, I turned back to race walking to ignite the healthy me. Running helped me kick asthma to the curb. I took the necessary steps to get rid of other health issues too. The most damaging issue was and still is gluten intolerance. Positive comments encouraged me to never give up and share my story.

Compliments that Lifted

I have heard many positive comments throughout my life, such as:
- You have a lot of God-given talent and abilities.
- You are intelligent, beautiful, and thin.
- I think you would be great at being an entrepreneur; I believe in you Annette.
- You have the power to change the world, one woman at a time.
- You are sitting on a gold mine; let's explore this further.

While on vacation an elderly man asked for my autograph. He thought I was Eva Longoria. You look like Eva Longoria. What a compliment to be considered as beautiful as her. I have had many people offer sincere compliments that lifted me and inspired me. Kind words can really make a difference in someone's life. Remember, you are only one conversation away from changing someone's life forever.

"Throughout my life, I learned to lead myself to find the true leader within me." ~Annette Marie Moore

Confidence Killers and Ten Remedies

If you have been affected by bullying in your lifetime, you know the internal scaring that takes place. I want to encourage you to find a balance in your life so you can be completely healthy. Here are ten remedies that will help you feel more confident in your shoes. You are worth it!

1. *Being Bullied.* Your remedy is to give others attention and lift someone in their struggle, or someone you believe has also been bullied. By showing your compassion to others, you are always able to find your own strength.

2. *Being Called Skinny.* Don't try to overcompensate and eat too much just because someone said you were skinny, but don't fall into an eating disorder either. Ask for emotional support.

3. *Being Called Fat.* Always know that what others see in you, is just their opinion. You know the difference between being obese and overweight. Take steps to regulate, without punishment.

4. *Being Called Stupid.* Remember that there is no measurement for true intellect. The best thing you can do here is to step away from that person.

5. *Shamed in Public or on Social Media.* A human behavior that is killing humanity is shaming. It is important to forgive and forget. Let it go. Remember, you are always good enough.

6. *Feeling Broke.* Poverty is a cruel mindset. To defeat it, you can go buy something just for you. Responsible spending allows more to flow to you.

7. *Feeling not Smart Enough.* This one is easy, take one hour a week and Google a topic you want to know more about or take 30 minutes a day to read a book. What comes up for you? There is nothing you cannot learn.

8. *Feeling Guilty*. Many women feel guilty when they go off their diet, eat the wrong foods, or don't move or exercise. To ease this feeling, celebrate every one of your micro-successes.

9. *Food Sneaking*. Did you raid the freezer and eat all the ice cream last night? You must allow yourself permission to make wise choices every day.

10. *Self-Hate*. Saving this for last because many women have deep self-hate. The guilt, shame, bullying, and low self-confidence has spiraled them into a black-hole. The only way to reverse this is through the mirror. Pick it up every day and look into your own eyes. Say, "I Love You." Reassure yourself that, "Everything is going to be okay." A sense of humor also plays an important part. Look at yourself naked in the mirror 15 minutes a day; learn to laugh and smile at yourself!

As an advocate for the total wellness of women, it's easier to prevent a chronic disease than it is to live with it and hope for a cure, spending a lot of money in the process. To truly lead in your own experience, you must develop confidence in your shoes. What old shoes are hanging around in your closet that you need to let go of and replace? What shoes do you want to continue to wear proudly as you walk throughout your life? Take smalls calculated steps towards your goals each day! Be Blessed!

AUTHOR ANNETTE MARIE MOORE

Annette Marie Moore is a promoter and speaker about women's health, who believes your health is your most important asset. She has been a runner since age nine, running track, cross country and road races. She has taught men's aerobics, worked with many personal trainers, and was a medical assistant for a podiatrist.

Annette recently moved to Orlando, Florida and has a daughter, Amy who lives in Atlanta, Georgia. Amy is the reason she gets out of bed every day.

Her business management degree from Mercer University, Atlanta, Georgia, co-mingled with being physically active, her love for cooking, and eating healthy have been assets throughout her adult life. Women ask her all the time about her secrets to good health and she is willing to share them. Having overcome several health issues, she has more information to add to her arsenal as she is passionate about helping women kick the diet mentality and adopt a wholehearted, healthy lifestyle to slow the aging process.

Her next partnership is publishing *Chocolate & Diamonds for the Woman's Soul*, Volume Three, scheduled February 14, 2018.

Connect with the Author. . .

Website

www.AnnetteMarieMoore.com

www.NeoLifeClub.com/AnnetteMoore

Phone: (352) 409-3086

"A leader embodies authenticity, integrity, and honor, knowing their inner calling and all they stand for in the world and can always see light even in the darkest moments." ~ Jennifer Elizabeth Masters

The Reluctant Leader

JENNIFER ELIZABETH MASTERS

For over twenty years I had an internal calling. *You must write a book about the trauma from childhood.* I stuffed the feelings and urges until the noise became unbearable. *Who on earth would want to hear about that horrible story?* became my common mental refrain.

Plenty, apparently. The voices in my head soon became real and caused me to take action toward releasing this part of my story. Standing in my own integrity, I finally said YES!

My first book, *Odyssey Victim to Victory*, wasn't a best seller, and it wasn't even a money maker. It did, however, help me become an expert in healing trauma. I overcome depression, anxiety, Fibromyalgia, Epstein Barr auto-immune disease, intense fears, illness, and codependency, AND I overcame every addiction imaginable. I didn't do a twelve-step program. I created the system to do it myself.

If I could do it for myself, I certainly could help others as well. Telling my story took tremendous courage. I asked my guides, "Could I wait until after my mother dies?"

The response was a distinct, *No!*

There had to be a reason my mother needed to hear my story. I reluctantly mailed my published work to her. For over a year we barely spoke.

Eventually, she cooled down enough to ask the tough question, "Did you really feel I didn't love you?"

Afterward she admitted to wanting to sue me for liable. Fortunately for me, telling the truth isn't libelous.

Once my story was published and my internal silence broken, all my life secrets were revealed; which gave me a sense of freedom I never thought possible. All the guilt and shame I endured for over half my life dissipated. True, I had to face my mother after making her sound like *Mommy Dearest*. Telling the truth gave me the courage to face the world. Publishing *Odyssey* opened the door for me to meet many men and women who have endured the same situation.

I admit that I put this book off for a very long time. I wasn't the only naysayer that impeded my progress, however. My youngest child was incredulous that I could call myself a relationship coach when I had four divorces to my credit. My daughter's criticism of my vocation made me reassess. Instead of quitting, I used what I learned to write articles to guide others. I didn't know all, but my wisdom was erudite.

I knew what didn't work. I had experienced every kind of abuse known to woman. I had learned compassion, patience, and understanding. In overcoming my personal trauma, demons, and fears I learned systems that I could repeat to help others heal their trauma and low self-esteem so they, too could be happy no matter what.

I found my intuitive gifts were a tremendous asset in coaching. Instead of doing energy clearing for some, I recognized how people were transforming; I used it for everyone.

The unique coaching model I was creating, became vortexes of empowerment and love. I could see people's issues at the root. I heard what they needed. People who were depressed weren't any longer. Suicidal issues and drug addictions were cleared. Women who came to me hating their husbands found they loved them more after working with me than they did when they first married.

A woman from India read one of my blog posts and said she knew that I could help save her from an arranged marriage. Her father had given her a time limit to find a man on her own. If she wasn't able to find love he would do it for her. She was a doctor and well-educated woman. She wanted to marry for love, unlike her parents before her. I wondered what on earth I was getting myself into? Was I doing match-making too?

Doubts surfaced. I wondered why on earth this woman contacted me? How could I possibly help someone across the world find love?

I knew how to manifest. I had manifested a brand-new car, a house and several men for myself (not at the same time, I might add). I had learned how to be happy alone which was no small feat for this formerly needy, codependent woman. Didn't that count for something? I knew that God and the universe wouldn't send me anything I couldn't handle. I pulled up my big girl panties and stepped up to the challenge that the universe put in my path.

I told her to break up with the man she was dating. I knew that having a boyfriend she didn't love was keeping her from meeting someone new. She was so committed to the process, she did as I asked and within two weeks met her new man. After several dates, she knew he was the one. He was handsome. He was also Indian with a successful business in the United States. The only drawback was that he had a girlfriend back in Virginia.

He indicated he would break up with her, they had been in a holding pattern for over two years. He wasn't happy and she couldn't possibly be either. He returned to take care of both his personal and professional business.

My client panicked and wanted to call him fearing she would lose the man she loved. She finally found her man, and she was sure he would run back into the arms of his girlfriend in Virginia. I had a vision of my client and her guy married. I knew she needed to rest in knowing he loved her. I couldn't share my vision with her. For over two months she cried, and worried. Each week I cleared another level of insecurity for her. I urged her to trust the process of life and focus on her patients in her office. We spoke often. In late November, he returned with a marriage proposal, and then the work began in earnest.

His mother was manipulative and clingy with her only son. She rejected his fiancé forcefully. My client returned to me for another session. I asked for guidance and saw that I needed to clear the relationship between mother and son and any past lives between the two women. As if by magic the mother's hold on her son weakened. She acquiesced and decided that my client was the perfect woman and began to embrace her and the idea of marriage.

In January 2013, they were married. Though I was invited to their celebratory bash, I had a daughter I couldn't leave alone in her final year of high school. The following summer the newlyweds visited my daughter and I for lunch when I got a glimpse of new life forming within my client. She smiled at me knowing I knew something. I tried valiantly to keep my vision secret. Within weeks of their return to India she confirmed that they were expecting their first child. Since that time, the two have created workshops for children to teach and share higher consciousness learning. Their second child was born in 2015.

Since 2013, other women and men have come to me presenting with issues of abandonment from childhood which perpetuates the same issue in adult relationships. After clearing the issue, I have guided many to step out of what feels like home to embrace the uncomfortable which in the end results in a healthy, balanced relationship. Home isn't necessarily what we want to attract in our love interests when it wasn't healthy for us as children.

In 2012, I was guided to write a book about sex, another stretch and departure for me. *Orgasm for Life* continues to sell well and is about to be translated into Spanish. Though my doubts about the role

I play as a healer, sex, and relationship coach have diminished, stepping into a more public persona has worn the heels off several pairs of shoes figuratively.

> Teaching Moment: Resistance will always come up. Offering daily astute guidance on social media can become a drag. Knowing what and when to outsource allows me time to focus on the things I love that brings me dollars and I help more people. Our old patterns and concerns about how we might be perceived can't be the stars that guide us.

I continue to stretch myself leaping before I am ready and writing without concern about whether anyone will read what I write. I always ask for guidance first and know that it is never wrong. I continue to be surprised about the new opportunities that present themselves to me as I follow my heart rather than my head and listen to my intuition. There will always be those who knew us before we were successful who continue to say, "You do what for a living?" Ignore the naysayers. They have no idea what kind of fire burns within that steers our course on the darkest of days.

I trust and follow my instinct with clients whether they get angry with me or not. I tell them the truth as gently as I can without judgment. I have been where they are and I remember all too well how I felt when others gave me suggestions. I thought I knew what was best for me, I didn't. Though I may be a little further down the path than others, it doesn't make me any better than anyone else. A compassionate leader knows that our true purpose is to encourage and guide rather than browbeat or diminish.

> Teaching Moment on Leadership: Being a leader means we recognize our wisdom but know we are all created equally. No one is better than another. I have lost clients because I spoke the truth. Years later they reappear and apologize for having their head where it couldn't see the light of day. Egos are like that. We think we're right and everyone is out to get us until we recognize it is the other way around.

People want to be around us when we are loving, nonjudgmental, and encouraging. Why wouldn't they? Leaders offer insight and help others to find the courage to do what seems incongruent or foreign. We help people find their inner voice and strength like we did. Stepping outside the box for us is what we do after all we are the ones that burned the box and ate the crumbs that marked the path back to safety so that we had to go all the way to the finish line.

Leaders offer a listening ear, a shoulder to lean on, and the encouragement to go the distance when resistance stops you cold. True leaders shine the light of infinite possibilities for those who are uncertain. Their footsteps are sure even on the rocky incline. If one way has a dead end, they quickly regroup and find a better path. Leaders are unafraid to be different and see criticism as a gift to betterment. They know in their hearts their path is illuminated by the stars.

AUTHOR JENNIFER ELIZABETH MASTERS

For over a decade Jennifer has empowered thousands of men and women find love, passion and happiness in their lives and relationships helping them heal co-dependency, addictions, depression, anxiety, suicidal tendencies, fears and suffering. Some of her clients have been, producers, spiritual leaders and authors. Wayne Dyer was not only a client but also a friend.

Jennifer is an author, certified love and happiness coach, Hypnotherapist, Neurolinguistic Programming Practitioner, a Master Energy Healer, ordained minister, and mother of three spiritually grounded adults.

She has been a featured author on *Digital Romance, Your Tango* and *MindBody Network* and been interviewed over 300 times on *Blogtalk, Voice America* and *BBS*.

Jennifer's personal healing journey from trauma has taken her all around the world from the UK, Europe, India, Bali and across the United States and Canada. And from Master Gardener owning her own landscape design business, *For Heaven Scapes, Ltd.* for eleven years to the person she is today, a fearless woman who radiates compassion and authenticity.

What her clients like best about her is that she listens without judgment, is completely present and is highly tuned into the Divine and
Universal which profoundly assists her clients with their process exactly where they are trying to get clarity.

Jennifer has authored over 950 articles and three books. *Happy Anywhere! The Guide For Overcoming Anxiety, Depression and Unhappiness,* is due to be published in late fall 2017.

Jennifer healed her own auto-immune disease, tumors, depression,
anxiety and Fibromyalgia. She shares her insights about how our mind
creates stories that keep us from happiness.

Connect with the Author. . .

Website: http://www.JenniferElizabethMasters.com
Social Media
　　Facebook: https://www.facebook.com/JenniferElizabethMasters/
　　Twitter: https://twitter.com/JeniferEMasters
　　Instagram: https://www.instagram.com/jenniferelizabethmasters/

"Following your dream—that is freedom. Even when it's hard or scary, following your heart's passion feels right and purposeful. A leader opens doors to dreams that we may step through and share the vision." ~ Caz

What Does Your Writing Reveal About You as a Leader?

CAZ

*T*he ability to write with clarity and objectivity is a critical skill for any leader. Solid writing garners respect. Organization and structure when forming your words leads readers into your message; people listen to what you say when it's well-written.

Poor writing saps your credibility. Whether this perception is fair or not, the reality is that bad writing directly damages personal, professional, and business brands.

When you scribe a quick email message, or craft a full-length professional journal article, or a chapter in a book, you reveal yourself in what you write; in the nuances and choices you make. Crafting the best word choice, creating organization and variety in sentence structure, selecting an appropriate tone, including references that speak to the reader—these interlocking pieces form the leader's message and communicate her vision to the world.

What Does Your Writing Say About You?

The written message is one-dimensional. This is a fact that is often experienced as a hard-learned lesson when an email (or a string of email messages), blows up in our face. Misunderstanding, confusion, and miscommunication are common when words alone carry the burden to communicate.

Are you surprised to realize that, even in one-dimension, your writing may reveal secrets you'd rather keep under wraps? Your written message may contain clues that leap off the page and carry the potential to undercut your effectiveness.

Style

Writing style is often an extension of leadership style and says a great deal about personality in general. How do you use pleasantries and personal pronouns? Do you use passive voice? Do you choose pretentious words like utilize instead of use?

A writing style that removes pleasantries and personal pronouns and uses passive voice sounds formal and stiff. Pleasantries include phrases and words like: please, thank you, appreciation, asking about a current situation, and good wishes for an upcoming holiday.

How (and how often) you use pronouns is a key component of writing style. The inclusion or absence of pronouns such as: you, I, me, we, us, he, she, they, reveals more than most writers realize.

Your voice does show up in writing. Choosing to use passive voice or active voice is especially revealing of your leadership and personality styles. For example:

- Passive voice reads like this: *Information should be forwarded to my office.*
- Active voice reads like this: *Please forward this information to my office.*

The King (or Queen) Rules Here!

Do you include questions in your writing? Do you address your audience directly to solicit opinions, feedback, and input? How you deliver your message reveals your leadership style. For example, if you rarely ask questions, likely you operate with yourself at the top and most communication flows one way—from the leader downward.

Writing that is filled with decisions and directives rather than explanations and data shows little regard for the reader's need to understand the reasoning behind those decisions. Such writing reveals an autocratic leadership style and reflects a low level of trust in your follower's ability to handle information appropriately.

A largely unconscious demonstration of superiority (one that is seen more often in female writers than male) is unusual punctuation and formatting. For example, excessive use of bold, several words or phrases written in all capitals, or negatives underlined as if the reader is too dumb to understand and decide which words are important. What is truly unfortunate about this writing style is that it's easily corrected by someone gently explaining to the writer how patronizing and disrespectful it is for both the writer and the reader. Good writing does not need this kind of emphasis added.

Frustration or Anger

"I repeat: Do NOT staple this form when you submit it!

Have you ever included a sentence like this in an email? Anger, frustration, and arrogance all show up in writing in several ways. What I spot most often are pompous language or hot words and phrases such as: unfair, poor judgment, excuse, complaint, retaliatory. The unusual punctuation habits I mentioned above can also be an indication of arrogance. The words you choose show your disdain, or your warmth and support. Which do you show? It's your choice and one that I highly recommend be intentional.

The pieces of written communication come together like a jigsaw puzzle. To translate your vision from your mind into a written format that clearly communicates your message is challenging and can be time-consuming. The effort is worthwhile. Every leader should be intentional and transparent when crafting written messages.

Ensure that your written words:

- **Embed your vision and culture across a wide audience.**
  Effective writing provides consistent interaction with others. Committing your vision to words spreads its reach, both internally and externally.

  When you write well, you humanize your brand and enable others to make it their own. This recruits and engages talent, partners, and customers to your vision.

- **Are available for study and revision.**
  Leaders who consider themselves above feedback won't lead for long.

  Writing is intensely personal, which makes it easy to feel intimidated by critique. Leaders solicit critique rather than avoid it. Your message will be strengthened when you are open to receiving feedback.

  Every word written has the potential to spark discussion, and that open dialog may be exactly what triggers your next big idea. Good writing empowers leaders and those we lead.

- **Reflect Author-ity.**
  Writing enables you to lead the conversation in your industry as a leading authority. Publish insightful written content to position yourself as a thought leader in your industry and scale your influence. Great writing skills allow you to stand out from the crowd.

- **Enable you to hold others accountable**
  Give people a standard that they can reference. It is easier to hold people accountable for something that you've communicated in writing.

  Hold yourself and others responsible to your written message to align efforts toward the same goal.

- **Clarify your thoughts and reveal your subconscious.**
  The act of writing is in itself clarifying; it gives a leader the chance to privately develop their way of looking at problems in a way that can be communicated to others.
  Writing allows leaders to convey their instinctive knowledge to others. When we write out the thoughts behind our instincts, this enables us to more easily, and intentionally, replicate our skills in others.
- **Remove fear.**
  Writing is a great tool for leaders to use when struggling with troubling question or problem. The act of writing out your thoughts allows your mind to explore alternatives that were not obvious or hidden behind emotion.

  As Stephen King says, "*Good writing is...about letting go of fear and affectation.*" There are plenty of fears in life that cannot be easily handled. Writing is not one of them. Writing puts ego on the line. And leaders let go of ego and move forward.
- **Attract influencers.**
  Influential people will align themselves with your brand when you write well—both as a favor to you and because they see you as an asset for their brand.

I hesitate to say it's all about image, however to a certain degree, it is. Charisma, charm, credibility, appeal, humility—these are words commonly chosen to describe a leader's characteristics. And they have in common an underlying concern with image and perception.

Writing Transcends Gender

This premise of this book centers around women leaders who break the glass ceiling mindset. Historically, women writers have been leaders—largely because their voice was not otherwise heard. Countless times women, even into today, have taken on a male pen-name. Several well-known examples come to mind. literary sisters Charlotte, Emily, and Anne Brontë first published their works under the male pseudonyms of Currer, Ellis, and Acton Bell. A little more recently, J.K. Rowling used ambiguous initials because her publisher thought the target young male audience would be put off by a book written by a woman. Even more recently, James Chartrand, successful blogger under *Men With Pens*, revealed her gender and continues to use the pseudonym.

Is it necessary for a woman to write as a man today? Not at all. I believe that James Chartrand does herself, and women writers in general, a disservice by continuing to use the pseudonym. I totally get why she has chosen to continue with her brand and do not fault her for this choice. Rather, I encourage women writers to step into their leadership role by fully embracing and using our feminine gender. We need all our voices to wield a power that we have not fully developed. We have the power to destroy the glass ceiling by refusing to acknowledge its existence.

Writing as a leadership skill is often overlooked; this is an oversight that I find difficult to understand. An effective leader—everyone will agree—must communicate their vision to those they lead and to the world in general. Image shapes perception. Perception is currency. To a leader, currency is counted in followers, in team members to be led, and in people who share the leader's vision.

There is an immense payoff to you, as a leader, when you improve your writing skills. There is an even bigger payoff to you as a woman when you join your voice with others and embrace that you truly are *Conceived to Lead*.

AUTHOR CAZ

CaZ (that's pronounced Kay-Zee) is a writer and coach with a purpose and a passion. She is the Writer Success Coach and follows her vocation to guide writers to become authors.

Candy Zulkosky became CaZ when she left the safety of trading hours for dollars and took up a career as a freelance technical writer, ghost writer, and tech diva just in time to be part of the revolutionary changes print on demand brought to publishing. Two of her books, Purpose Powered People and Purpose to Author-ity, share aspects of this journey and explain how you can find and follow your own story and passion to become a published author. A third book, A Daybook for Writers: Transforming Writers into Authors, offers creative prompts and insight from authors to encourage writers to enjoy a daily writing habit.

> *"Every author is unique, and tells their singular story in the books we write and publish together."* ~CaZ, the Writer Success Coach

Today, I live at the beach on an island in North Carolina where I appreciate living my dream to be a successful author who supports other writers in finding their success.

I continue to add to my 35+ years of experience and serve writers as the Writer Success Coach, a 100K Impact Certified Business and Leadership Coach, owner of Manifest Publishing, and founder of BizCardBooks.

My joy is transforming writers into authors. I'm often asked what the difference is between a writer and an author. The simple answer is an author is published. And yet, becoming an author goes beyond publication and includes embracing an author's mindset. Exploring your answer to what it means to be an author is a fun part of coaching with me.

In addition to coaching and publishing services, writers benefit from my extensive background in training through my boot camps, masterminds, and a master courses.

The exclusive *Book Writer Success Boot Camp* gives you the motivation and inspiration to finish, taking you from book idea to completed manuscript in 90 days AND gets you ready to publish with all your questions answered and decisions made about how you will move your manuscript from written to published.

In the powerful *Publish-it Now! Boot Camp*, we take the next step together to get your book published, breaking down the complex publishing process into easily accomplished pieces.

In *Beyond Your Book* we bring it all together, taking 12 weeks to guide writers from first draft to finished manuscript; and publish your book; and build your author's platform; and launch your book marketing campaign.

And for those who prefer an all-inclusive option, choose from ghost writing, editing, book design, all-in-one book packages or perhaps our signature *BizCardBooks* option.

With *BizCardBooks*, coaches, entrepreneurs, business owners, speakers—anyone who presents a message to the public—gains a complete publishing team to get your book written and into your hands. Unlock your vision and bring your message to the world. A *BizCardBook* is a small, laser-focused and impactful book that gives life to your story and enables you to embrace your greatness by stepping into your dream of being an author.

"My joy is transforming writers into authors." ~CaZ, Writer Success Coach

Connect with the Author. . .

Book a complimentary consultation time with CaZ by scheduling time on her calendar: https://bookme.name/writersuccesscoach

Website

http://www.thewritersuccesscoach.com
http://www.manifestpublishing.com

Social Media

Facebook: https://www.facebook.com/CaZWriterSuccessCoach
LinkedIn: https://www.linkedin.com/in/candyzulkosky/
Twitter: https://twitter.com/candysbytes

Programs

Business Card Books: http://www.bizcardbooks.com
Book Writer Boot Camp: http://www.bookwritersuccess.com
Publishing Boot Camp: http://www.publishitnowbootcamp.com

"*This is the ultimate chicken and the egg situation. The chicken: Women will tear down the external barriers once we achieve leadership roles... The egg: We need to eliminate the external barriers to get women into those roles in the first place. Both sides are right.*"

~ Sheryl Sandberg, Lean In: Women, Work, and the Will to Lead